Give
GOD SOMETHING
HE CAN
Feel

A 30 DAY DEVOTIONAL CHALLENGE
FOR DEVOTED CHRISTIANS

J.L TURNER

WestBow
PRESS
A DIVISION OF THOMAS NELSON

WestBow Press books may be ordered through booksellers or by contacting:

WestBow Press
A Division of Thomas Nelson
1663 Liberty Drive
Bloomington, IN 47403
www.westbowpress.com
1-(866) 928-1240

Scriptures for Daily Readings, as well as in the content of this book, are taken from the King James Version of The Holy Bible.

ISBN: 978-1-4497-8577-2 (sc)
ISBN: 978-1-4497-8576-5 (hc)
ISBN: 978-1-4497-8578-9 (e)

Library of Congress Control Number: 2013903251

Printed in the United States of America

WestBow Press rev. date: 3/29/2013

TABLE OF CONTENTS

DEDICATION

First, and above all, I give thanks to the God of my Salvation. I also wish to thank my wife Aisha Turner, as well as to my pastor and mentor, Bishop Jerome H. Ross Sr. and Dr. I.T. Bradley. Heartfelt gratitude to my parents, both spiritual and natural, to my "hater," I pray God continues to bless you so you can keep pushing me. Last but not least Reverend Charles Runion; I have only experienced two teachers that went above and beyond for me and because of your efforts this project is possible.

Also, I want to thank the readers for your support, as the financial profits from this book will be earmarked for the furthering of the cause of Christ in both the literary and oration form of this ministry. As God allows, we plan to produce more material for the perfecting of the saints and the edifying of the body of Christ.

PREFACE

This book is the culmination of the preaching and teaching ministry of Evangelist Jamar L. Turner. The nuggets and gems you will find in these pages have been life changing and transforming for myself as well as others, as I have counseled and preached in the Church and behind prison walls. I pray these are as life changing, instrumental, and uplifting in your life as they have been in mine.

Growing as a believer and in intimacy with God is a journey you must take day by day. While you might be tempted to read ahead due to the brevity of this material, I encourage you to savor each and every word carefully and to take small bites at a time. Read, savored, and properly used, these words, along with the suggested scriptures, will feed and nurture your devotional life each day for thirty days.

This devotional is designed not only to build and nurture a devotional life in the believer, but also to challenge you to be ever growing and always maturing. There is a challenge included with every devotional so that you may apply it to your daily walk with God. This will also help you grow spiritually and live a life that is more pleasing to God. The goal here is for you to develop a more intimate relationship with Him. This can only be done through self-denial, love for your brothers and sisters in Christ, prayer, repentance, devotion, and submission to the Spirit.

This book is also designed to help believers in a social aspect, equipping you to deal with neighbors, family, friends, and even enemies. We cannot continue to claim we are "spiritual" if we are socially inadequate. We cannot claim we are in love with God if we do not have the love of Christ for our neighbor. One repetitive theme you will find throughout this book is: "You will never be any closer to God than you are to your brother." Likewise, your human relationships can be a hindrance to your spiritual intimacy.

FOREWORD

Astronomers regularly scan the stars and the universe observing the planets in our solar system. In 1846, the planet Neptune was discovered by William Lassell. A surprise to astronomers over the next 150 years was the number of moons surrounding the planet (13 in total).

Christians read devotional books to help them with their spiritual maturity. I recommend Rev. Jamar Turner's contribution to this field. It is written to help the believer in Christ to grow in wisdom and knowledge. The Christian may think, "Oh, another devotional book ..." My belief is that inside these pages you will discover "many moons." Throughout the individual lessons, there are insights from the Word and recommendations for action that will increase the believer's devotion to God and improve their relationship with others.

It is the kind of writing that can be read more than once and the reader will learn something new each time. It is similar to the discovery of the thirteen moons around Neptune. They were not discovered immediately because the various moons would be hidden by darkness or closeness to the planet itself. With each devotional reading, the daily lessons will reveal something important about God and something about the reader himself. Truths will be revealed as light shines forth in the dark corners of our personal life and a closeness to God is being cultivated.

Enjoy your own discovery as you read and meditate upon Rev. Turner's message in **"Give God Something He Can Feel ... A devotional challenge for a devoted Christian."**

Charles Runion
Winter 2013

DAY 1

Giving God your all

DAILY READING:
Philippians 3:8; John 14:22-23; Hebrews 12:6

*I beseech you therefore, brethren, by the mercies of God, that
ye present your bodies a living sacrifice, holy, acceptable
unto God, which is your reasonable service.*
—ROMANS 12:1

*For lo, they that are far from thee shall perish: thou hast destroyed all them
that go a whoring from thee. But it is good for me to draw near to God:
I have put my trust in the Lord God, that I may declare all thy works.*
—PSALM 73:27-28

THE GREATEST OFFERING OR SACRIFICE we can give to God is ourselves. We are in a covenant relationship and we are serving a personal, relational God. Despite what scientists and theorists may say, he is a God that is mindful of man (Psalm 8:4) and wants a deeper intimacy with his creation. So, even in suffering, we prove our devotion to God in being a sacrifice as he was a sacrifice. Do you think you can be fully devoted without some pain and sacrifice? This is how we respond to a God that loves us so much that he gave his only begotten (John 3:16). Just as the love in a marriage is finalized once the two parties have presented their bodies, we do the same for God in the furthering of our intimacy with Him.

Paul defines this as the very least we can do: our *reasonable service*. In many other translations this "reasonable service" is even translated to our "reasonable worship" or the very least we can render to God. Wouldn't it be something, if God was so pleased with your life that the way you lived became worship unto him? What if our lives were an aspect of the spiritual and truthful worship in which he requires of us in this last hour (John 4:23)?

He also qualifies how we should present ourselves. The Apostle states, we are to present ourselves "holy" and "acceptable" unto God. This is in reference to the sanctifying of a believer, or his setting apart. This will be a sacrifice because you must give up what is natural to you to please a God who is super-natural. These qualifications are necessary because there are those that will present themselves, but not in the manner in which God is requiring. For example, the Bible states that when the sons of God came, "Satan came also among them to present himself" (Job 2:1). We do not present ourselves as devils, but rather as living sacrifices, holy and acceptable unto God. In this way, our relationship with God is literally brought into its fullness with sacrifice. He sacrificed His Son for us, and in response, we are to sacrifice ourselves. However, we are blessed in that we are sacrificed alive.

What does it mean to be sacrificed alive? Christ was a dead sacrifice and has paved the way for us to be living sacrifices. In essence, it means we must sometimes endure hardship and suffering for the sake of molding our character. This may also mean that we embrace some self-denial and selflessness that we would be pleasing to God. It also means that we "know him in the fellowship of his suffering and in the body of this death" (Philippians 3:10). The Psalmist says, " …I have put my trust in God that I may declare all his works." In His sovereignty, He holds the right to take us through whatever is necessary to move us where He wants us to be in our relationship with Him. In this we will suffer, but the suffering is a result of true mercy and not true justice. If God were executing true justice, then we would all be worthy of death (Romans 6:23); even in our affliction and when evil comes upon us. St. Augustine suggests that, in the all knowingness of God, he allows evil so that he may be able to bring good even from evil or suffering.

The challenge for us is to be a people of God that are not only holy and acceptable unto God but in the world and in trial and in trouble. Your neighbor should experience the goodness of God through your goodness towards them. We are to be a people in whom He can manifest His divine work, regardless of the cards life may deal us. While He is working through us, we need to know that afflictions may come for the sake of His ultimate glory.

For example, I am a brain tumor survivor so I know what it is to live with what people have died. I am aware of having to be dependent upon medication to live a normal life but in never turning away from him and yielding my life and body to him in hard circumstances, God has blessed me supernaturally. He took me off medication that the doctor said I would be dependent upon for the rest of my life: with no complications! He allowed me to be a Dean's list student and published author, when I was once qualified because of my handicap to be a slow learner. I say all this to say: give yourself to God regardless of what it cost you and He will give back!

Your Challenge for Day 1:

If you are going to know Him, we may have to suffer, but the believer who suffers is worthy of reigning. Your challenge today is to realize that what you are facing may not be about you at all. You cannot quit because someone needs you. If not for someone else, perhaps it is a lesson to be learned for self that will help you be better to the people you may encounter in the future. No matter what kind of trouble comes your way, you are called upon to be someone God can trust to trust Him, someone God can charge with the task of giving Him all the glory, even when your life doesn't seem so glorious.

DAY 2

Giving God your all, Part II

DAILY READING:
Romans 13:10; Psalm 73:27-28;Ephesians 1:4; Matthew 22:37-40

I beseech you therefore, brethren, by the mercies of God, that
ye present your bodies a living sacrifice, holy, acceptable
unto God, which is your reasonable service.
—ROMANS 12:1

BELIEVER'S ARE TO BE PRESENTED holy and acceptable unto God. This is the least we can do with ourselves. This means the least of God's children should be holy and acceptable.

Being "holy" means we are consecrated and set apart for His service. This requires that we be holy in the sense of spiritual maturity. This means that we should carry ourselves in way that we do not behave as babes in Christ but rather those that walk with God. In one sense, we are to be unblemished.

By this I mean that there are certain things that should not be named among you as believer of God. There are some things that simply shouldn't show up on our spiritual resumés. There are some things as a believer you should refuse to experience, no matter how much the world imposes it on us. Why? Because after we try those things, we will never be the same. The things that are most pleasing to the flesh are often the most destructive to the spirit, and once we try them, we may never want to try Jesus again. This is the loss that you may never recover from. My Pastor always reminds us, "if you lose everything and still have Jesus you have enough to start all over." To live life self absorbed and self-indulged will cost you not only Jesus but also those other things that you cherish so dearly. The works of the flesh (Galatians 5:19-21) will leave you in debt, divorced, alone and unhappy. But being pleasing to God will not only land you a blessing to your home and Church, but, more importantly, you will be blessed because God is satisfied with you.

Sometimes these blessings may not be material; they may be spiritual. If you deny yourself a carnal or fleshly experience, you may just gain a spiritual experience. God can be the experience of a lifetime. If you are chasing that next adventure or that next high, God can take you to higher heights and deeper depths.

We must remember that the pouring out of His Spirit is the best thing we will ever experience. As believers, we tend to lose focus and get lost in our search for that next high, even after we have tasted of all His goodness. Know that there is nothing and no one greater than God. No one will ever be a better asset in our lives or better influence upon our lives. If we are being honest with ourselves, we know we are free to try and do a lot of things in life, but a life without Him is not living at all.

On the other hand, plenty of us are holy and are trying to live a godly life, yet we are not acceptable. We may be Heaven-bound without being any good to anyone on Earth; sold out to God but selling everyone else out in the process. And this is unacceptable. An acceptable sacrifice is one that can be put in the place of sin and cause a relationship to continue. Jesus becomes our sacrifice that is put in the place of our sin and reconciles us to God. Likewise, our living sacrifice is our response to Christ's sacrifice and also in relation to our brother we stand in the way of his sin. Our calling is beyond us and even further than us - to affect the world.

We are called to be restorers, administering the ministry of reconciliation to those in a dying world. Scripture teaches us, "Be ye holy, but not blameful in love" (Ephesians 1:4) and also that "Love showeth no man ill" (Romans 13:10). We also have to be able to go to God on behalf of our brothers and sisters. When we do, He will accept us and hear our petitions. The Bible speaks of believers witnessing and praying for one another. "Confess *your* faults one to another, and pray one for another, that ye may be healed. The effectual fervent prayer of a righteous man availeth much" (James 5:16).Then we are even asked to sanctify one another (1 Corinthians 7:14). I say all this to say that, someone should be better because of the God in you.

Your Challenge for Day 2

As believers totally sold out for God, we are in the business of reconciliation and even sanctification. Because you have given yourself over to God and He has sanctified you, you likewise have the power to sanctify your home. Have you strived to sanctify your children? Your mate? Your friends, neighbors, and loved ones? Are you working to rebuild the connection between God and people? What are you willing to give up so that people will not miss out on meeting God? Are you your brother's keeper or his stumbling block, his biggest hurdle in this walk?

DAY 3

Love your enemies

DAILY READING:
Philippians 2:1-4; Romans 12:9-10; Proverbs 18:24; John 15:12-17

Ye have heard that it hath been said, "Thou shalt love thy neighbor and hate thine enemy," but I say unto you, love your enemies, bless them that curse you, do good to them that hate you, and pray for them which despitefully use you, and persecute you; That ye may be the children of your Father which is in Heaven: for He maketh His sun to rise on the evil and on the good, and sendeth rain on the just and on the unjust. For if ye love them which love you, what reward have ye? Do not even the publicans the same? And if ye salute your brethren only, what do ye more than others? Do not even the publicans so? Be ye therefore perfect, even as your Father which is in Heaven is perfect.
—MATTHEW 5:43-48

I HAVE DISCOVERED THAT IN ORDER to really be in love with God, you must at least have love for your neighbor, our brother, and your enemy. This love is the *"agape"* love and it means to esteem or take delight in. Even if the person's acts are displeasing you should be esteeming or delighting in them, knowing that God once looked beyond your faults and saw your needs. Jesus even qualifies this. In order for us to be His children, we must love our haters. We are also instructed to "bless them who curse you and do good to those who despitefully use you" (Luke 6:28). God knows this is no easy task, but it is what we are called to do as His children representing His love in the world.

As difficult as loving our enemies may be, Jesus managed to do it. He possessed the power to destroy anyone that was in His way but instead he cooperated with opposition, taught his adversaries, instructed those that hated him, and ultimately, because we all have been more enemy than friend - He gave us the opportunity to be saved. He did this, knowing those that oppose him who were also religious leaders were wrong and he still respected their traditions. He esteemed them and took delight in their way of righteousness (Matthew 5:20).

Although He sets the bar high, that does not give us an excuse to avoid this responsibility. We must strive to love as He did, bless as He did, and even pray as He did. This will require some work on your part. This is a job ahead of us in trying to be like Jesus and it will demand some energy, time, and effort but it is God's desire that we conform to the image of his Son (Romans 8:29). Our goal, this day and every day, is to become more like Jesus in all we do. The more we resemble Jesus in our walk with God, the closer we will be to God. This is to be like him even in the way we love God and one another, because this will affect all the other areas in which you strive to be Christ-like.

Without fail, we must absolutely love, even those who have ill intentions toward us. These "enemies" will become a motivator to move us toward our destiny. Even if we have not yet reached a place where we can truly love them, we should at least have an appreciation for them. Without them, many of us would not be as close to God as we are. They may be the very reason we learned to pray, to hold our tongue, and to submit to the Spirit. In many cases, our enemies have taught us to say "no" to ourselves and allow vengeance to be the Lord's. He prepares a table before us in the presence of our enemies (Psalms 23:5), so without the enemies there is no prepared table. Therefore whether you would like to admit it or not, your blessing maybe indirectly tied to your enemy.

We are also asked to "bless them." How? The answer is in service to the Lord whatever our ministry is. A preacher might preach a sermon that will inspire a spiritual breakthrough within them. A singer might perform a song that will strum the enemies' heartstrings and break through their disdain and anger toward the singer or the God they represent. We must be ready, willing, and able to serve even our enemies, because whether we want to admit it or not, God gave up His Son for them too. We are to pray for them—not *prey on* them, but *pray for* them. If we talk to God about them, He will make the relationship easier for us to handle. We must not forget that we are in the business of mending and restoring relationships because it is easier to live like Jesus if you love like Jesus.

YOUR CHALLENGE FOR DAY 3

As you grow more and more into what God wants you to be and follow in the footsteps of Christ, your challenge this day is to love your enemies. We may have contempt or deep issues with these people for past hurts, whether in word or deed, but as believers we must grow beyond these issues. This means you must mention your haters in your prayer life, consider them in your servanthood, and be kind and compassionate to them in Christian love—not only so that they might grow beyond whatever dislike they hold for you or the God in you, but also so you might prove yourself to be an acceptable and holy child of God.

DAY 4

Suffering as a common ground for relationship

DAILY READING:
Philippians 3:8, Revelation 3:20, 1 Tim 2:12, I Peter 4:1-2

That I may know Him, and the power of His resurrection, and the fellowship of His sufferings, being made conformable unto his death.
—PHILIPPIANS 3:10

When He heard this, Jesus said, "This sickness will not end in death. No, it is for God's glory so that God's Son may be glorified through it."
—JOHN 11:4

ARE YOU SUFFERING? ARE YOU facing trials and tribulations, big or small? If you are, I want to encourage you. We cannot be discouraged, for in the midst of suffering, God can become very real to you. In suffering, we can truly identify with Christ. I am not saying that your suffering is not very real nor am I trying to downplay what you are experiencing. But I do know that through the pain of suffering the presence of God is realized. We just have to keep our eyes and ears open to him until he comes to our deliverance.

There is some tension between God's love and His glory. There is a conflict here because we assume that because He loves us nothing bad could happen to us. But sometimes when God is trying to get some glory from you it may put you in an uncomfortable situation. For example, a good doctor puts needles in the back of an infant to inoculate them and without understanding what is happening, the infant just knows that he is in pain. God-inflicted pain is similar to this; he has both intention and purpose for all that we go through. It may not make sense now but as you grow and mature, you will realize it was a necessary struggle. God may inflict trials upon us for the sake of His glory, but this is not to say He does not love us.

Amongst the millions of reasons we suffer is because God must test us, and also in dealing with his glory we deal with God's heaviness or the pressure of God. It is this pressure that allows our lives to be glorious to God. Paul writes, " But we all, with open face beholding as in a glass the glory of the Lord, are changed into the same image from glory to glory, *even* as by the Spirit of the Lord." (1 Corinthians 3:18) We are changed as God is revealed. The hearers of that time also understood the pain of this process. We are also reminded in pain and affliction that, "Whom the Lord loveth He also chastiseth … (Hebrews 12:6).

Not only in affliction and this glory struggle are we transformed, but our commitment and love is also tested. Too often in struggle are we looking for the easy way out or some simple explanation. There may not be any basic explanation or easy way out for us other than to continue as the will of God permits. In the will of God *our* love must be tested, as His has already been put to the test in Jesus Christ and his sacrifice on Calvary. In any relationship where love exists, it must be tested and tried to prove its validity. The challenge for us is to give Him glory, even when it hurts. To prove ourselves to be a race of tested individuals that choose to love God in spite of the testing.

Also we must consider that there is "no new thing under the sun"

(Ecclesiastes 1:9), and all people of all times have gone through trials. Trials are scattered throughout the scriptures, even godly people suffered. Christ's dear friend, Lazarus, was allowed to die (John 11).Many others were born with or afflicted by blindness, ailments, and disorders. In our own lives, we have likely been "dealt a bad hand" time and again, but that says nothing about God's unending love for us. Jesus was not happy that Lazarus had died but he understood it was for the glory of God. The Bible records, "When Jesus therefore saw her weeping, and the Jews who had come with her, also weeping, He was deeply moved in spirit, and was troubled, and said, 'Where have you laid him?' They said, 'Lord, Come and see.' Jesus wept. And so the Jews were saying, 'Behold, how He loved Him!" (John 11:33-36).

We can and should take comfort in the fact that there is a method to this madness. Although we experience hardships for the sake of God's glory, we also experience blessings underserved. This is the love of God: it inflicted Christ so that we could be saved. This was His ultimate exhibition of love.

When we sin, it is a test of love, a measurement of how much we love ourselves versus how much we love our God. Can we love God even when it seems to be pointless? God allows bad things to sometimes happen to us so that we might come to better know His Son Jesus, that we might give Him glory. In turn, Christ can glorify His Father, and the Father may glorify the Son; then this glory will be shared with us. The Apostle Paul reminds us of this glorying we shall experience, "whom He foreknew, He predestined; whom He predestined, He called, whom He justified, He glorified" (Romans 8:29-30). So there is some glory for those that suffer with Christ.

When we speak of this glorying we are referring to an honor bestowed. We give God honor in our affliction on earth and he returns the honor in Heaven. Thus, we cannot lose sight of heaven or eternity when we suffer for Christ, because it will all make sense when we get there. This is momentary light affliction that we endure in comparison to all that God has for us. When we get to heaven, we will realize that we are better because of it. I say this to say that there is plenty of glory to be shared if we will only allow ourselves to be "vehicles of His glory" - here and now. It should not be our goal to continue in God's will for the sake of gaining honor but we will be glorified eventually.

We have the assurance that after we have known God in such a capacity, through the conflict and the testing, there will be no turning back! Paul said, "That I may know him, and the power of his resurrection, and the fellowship of his sufferings, being made conformable unto his death; If by any means I might attain unto the resurrection of the dead" (Philippians 3:11). So we are entering in a suffering for a relationship and companionship that will transcend time and move us into eternity. We need to enter in with a "by any means" in our spirit. We will miss the essence of who Jesus is if we fail to embrace suffering. If we open ourselves to seeing Christ in our trials and loving Him through the tests, we will notice that even our lowest state can be a revelation of just how big and how great our God really is. By comparison, we will recognize where we are in our relationship with Him.

YOUR CHALLENGE FOR DAY 4

Your challenge is to allow circumstance and opposition to reveal more of God to you. Instead of growing bitter, grow better ... in Him.

DAY 5

Survival of the Blessed

DAILY READING:
Isaiah 63:7-10, James 4:8-10, I Peter 4:1-2

And she spake out with a loud voice, and said, "Blessed art thou among women, and blessed is the fruit of thy womb."
—LUKE 1:42

FAR TOO OFTEN, WE ALLOW possessions and material things to determine whether we are blessed or not. In actuality, after we have been through all we have been through, if we still have peace of mind, a will to go on, and faith to stand on, we are truly blessed. We are blessed in the fact that in spite of the opposition we endure, we have a God to lean on. We have his smile we can borrow, his strength we can put on, and his peace when ours is broken. The Bible tells us that, "he was wounded for our transgressions, bruised for our iniquities, and the chastisement of our peace was upon him (Isaiah 53:5). He has taken it all on, so I am blessed when I don't feel it.

No matter how dysfunctional or scandalous our lives have been or become, we can still be blessed. The fact that God is willing to spare us, even as the sinners we are, is a great blessing in itself. Jesus also came from scandal and dysfunction, at least from a human perspective. For He was born to an unwed mother who was recently engaged at the time of His conception. He was a biological relative of Rahab, a prostitute. If Jesus Himself came from scandal, how can we expect to be exempt? If Jesus himself had to deal with dysfunctional families and poverty, how are we too good to experience it? He experienced this and he did not sin. At least in our lives we can look back and find some reasons that we should not be as blessed as we are. His record was clean; he was perfect from beginning to end.

Some of us have been born in dysfunctional families, broken homes, or homes without mothers and fathers but we can still know that God has considered us blessed. God declared His Son blessed in spite of His earthly ancestry. God said that Jesus was His Son in whom He was well pleased. Despite where he came from and because of this affirmation from his Heavenly Father, he is now a Son that can bless those who love and follow Him.

As men and women of God, we must be able to bless our homes and our children with nothing but our mere presence. We should be there and be active in the lives of our family members and friends. God made us a blessing not to be blessing to ourselves but others. We need to focus less on what we have (or lack) and more on who we are. If we take an honest look at whom we are and how far we have come, most of us can declare ourselves blessed. Our growth and survival ought to be the measuring sticks of our blessedness, not the car we drive or the label on the clothes we wear.

Sometimes the hand we are dealt is a truer measure of how blessed we actually are. For example, Jesus conquered sin, death, and the grave and is now sitting on the right hand of the Father; yet none of this is what declares Him blessed. No! Instead, what declares Him blessed is the fact that He began his earthly life in a humble stable, a barn. He started with "nowhere to lay His head" (Luke 9:58), a mere borrower and servant. For people to witness how far you have come is testimony to how much God has blessed your life. Too many of us become ashamed of our past or our humble beginnings. These are the clearest picture of what God can do. They should also be a reminder that just as He did it then, he can do it again.

Your Challenge for Day 5

The challenge today is to declare yourself blessed; regardless of your past and *because* of your future. You have made it through what would have sidetracked many, and because of that, you are a survivor and can testify to blessings others cannot.

DAY 6

My Life May Not Be Perfect, but It Is Pleasing

DAILY READING:
Romans 8:1; 12:2, II Corinthians 5:17

*Furthermore then we beseech you, brethren, and exhort you by
the Lord Jesus, that as ye have received of us how ye ought to walk
and to please God, so ye would abound more and more.*
—I THESSALONIANS 4:1

C.S LEWIS IN *MERE CHRISTIANITY*, one of the greatest Christian works of our time, suggests God is easy to please but hard to satisfy. This means that while he applauds our belief in his Son and loves our small attempts and efforts to be as he wants us to be, He is still looking for perfection and holiness. Not only is he looking for these, but he has made the way for us to obtain it.

This is the reason some of us never abound or make it to the top is because we are striving for perfection. This sets us up to constantly walk away discouraged with ourselves, feeling like failures. We can take heart in the fact that things will abound for us when our lives are pleasing to

God, even if they are not perfect. The Bible teaches us, "No good thing will He withhold from those who walk uprightly" (Psalm 84:11). Our perfection is obtainable only through Christ; and to attempt this of your own strength is to set yourself up for failure. Because he decided to be fully man and walk this walk out before us as fully God; we too have the ability to not make our own way in perfection but follow in His footsteps. Incarnation means that God has descended into the whole of the human condition. This means that he is not only aware of what our humanity gravitates toward; but also he knows it firsthand and was without sin.

Throughout the book of I Thessalonians, Paul encourages believers to strive for perfection in Christ. This perfection does not encompass being without fault or failure, but rather the happy medium of living a life that is pleasing to God. We should always be growing, and that means we will make mistakes; learning how to grow beyond our mistakes is the important part. We must also learn to take responsibility for the things we have done and said. The Christian thing to do when you have made a not-so-Christian decision is to be responsible for your actions. We must try our best to mend whatever we have broken, repent for all our sins, and love wherever we have hated. This will not make us perfect by any means, but it can mean the difference between one who is pleasing and one who is pretending.

There are two things about us that have a very special relationship with each other: our life and our walk. How we live our lives will determine our walk. What you feed yourself and what you entertain will determine how you conduct yourself. If we live a life of self-satisfaction, we will walk after the flesh. However, if we live a life of self-sacrifice, we will, "walk not after the flesh, but after the Spirit"(Romans 8:1). Sometimes we worry so much about life and missed opportunities when some of those opportunities may actually be snares that we are better off avoiding.

It is better to live an abounding life than a life bound. An abounding life is the rich life that only Jesus can provide. It is life not absent of trouble, but it is rich and full despite opposition. It is a life that will put us in the position to do more for Him in His service. On the other hand, when we live bound lives, we can still claim to know Christ, but you will belong to something else entirely because you are bound to it.

YOUR CHALLENGE FOR DAY 6

The challenge for you today is to strive for that abounding life, that practical perfection in Christ rather than in yourself. A life that is perfect in Christ is pleasing to God. To be perfect in Christ is to allow the mending of the life Christ lived and the life you live. To have a heart that is bent towards God. This requires you to allow Him to live through you. This is also how we know that we are serving a living, true God, for He lives in us.

DAY 7

My Life May Not Be Perfect, but It Is Pleasing, Part II

DAILY READING:
Psalm 73:27-28, James 4:8-10, Romans 6:1-10

*Furthermore then we beseech you, brethren, and exhort you by
the Lord Jesus, that as ye have received of us how ye ought to walk
and to please God, so ye would abound more and more.*
—I THESSALONIANS 4:1

A LIVING TESTIMONY IS NOT ABOUT honoring what you used to do
or what you used to be. Believers who do this are often guilty of
missing things that were not pleasing to God in the first place. We must
not be bitter when God requires us to give up a lifestyle or pleasure that is
not pleasing to Him. The born-again believer, bought with a price of His
death, purchased with his blood, can testify of God's goodness and His
greatness in the way they live and how they treat people.

These will become an exhibition, an outside show of what's going on
inside. This is our way to show to the world that we have been with God
and that we are enjoying a close relationship with Him. When we have

an intimate relationship with God, we will have a meaningful concern for all people and will hold ourselves to a higher moral standard of living. Because of our closeness with such perfection and holiness in God, we imitate as children what we see in him. Believers are called to "Be ye therefore followers of God, as dear children; And walk in love, as Christ also hath loved us, and hath given himself for us an offering and a sacrifice to God for a sweet smelling savor" (Ephesians 5:1-2). It is this intimacy with God that will separate us from things that are not like Him or liked by Him, for no one can have an intimate relationship with God without enjoying His company. When we enjoy His presence on that level, His ways and His plan for us will become our preferences in life. Then, you will gladly choose the godly way over the ungodly way; we will recommend righteousness over unrighteousness; we will choose justice over being unjust. Why? Because we will prefer the things of God and long to be like Him. This is not something we can discover overnight. It is a point we must grow to, for we are born in sin and "shapen in iniquity" (Psalm 51:5). What excites or entertains the flesh will be pleasurable to us until we get close to God.

We may never reach perfection, but living a life that is pleasing to God means we will not be comfortable with our many imperfections. It means we will be convicted by our vulnerabilities, our vices, and our guilty pleasures. This also means we need to take responsibility for our actions and make corrections and adjustments where necessary. We may have to repent to God or even to our brother or sister because of something we have said or done to hurt them.

Never forget that we are never any closer to God than we are to our brothers and sisters; therefore, we cannot live a pleasing life if you try to exclude or overlook them. Life cannot be walked independently. We will never make it through without depending on God and one another.

YOUR CHALLENGE FOR DAY 7

Your challenge today is to be pleasing, even though God looks beyond your faults and sees your needs. Do not allow His grace and mercy to be your handicap or your enablement. You have the power to say "no" to yourself and the strength to say "yes" to God. If you please Him, you will abound. Contrary to popular belief, you don't have to displease God to have a fun life or what most people deem to be good experiences. He will give you life and experiences in great abundance, a blessing He reserves for those who are His. Therefore, I challenge you to be pleasing in your walk, in your talk, and in your life, for you can be pleasing in the sight of God, through perfection in Christ, even if you are never absolutely perfect in His eyes.

DAY 8

How to handle the Hurt

DAILY READING:

I Peter 4:1-2, I Corinthians 15:31-34, Philippians 2:1-4

But when they came to Jesus, and saw that He was dead already, they brake not His legs: But one of the soldiers with a spear pierced His side, and forthwith came there out blood and water. And he that saw it bare record, and his record is true: and he knoweth that he saith true, that ye might believe. For these things were done, that the scripture should be fulfilled, "A bone of Him shall not be broken." And again another scripture saith, "They shall look on him whom they pierced."
—JOHN 19:33-34

DID IT HURT JESUS WHEN they pierced His side? You might be surprised to learn that it did not. Yes, it hurt Him to be beaten and bruised, to be ridiculed and humiliated, but it did not hurt Him to be pierced because He was already dead. Our flesh must die in order for us to deal with some of the betrayal and backstabbing that may come from those we love and trust. Like Jesus, whose death in the physical body prevented Him from feeling the pierce to His side, we also have to die to our flesh or our human responses to deal with whatever it is that our enemies do to us.

This death in which I am referring to is the death in which the Apostle Paul often referenced. More specifically, he stated that the mind that was set on the flesh was death but the mind that is set on the spirit is life and peace (Romans 8:6). So in a sense we have to die to, a deathly mindset or fleshly thought process. Notice the transition in his words once you have "died" to the flesh or set your mind to the Spirit. In this, you allow yourself to experience a life that is peaceful. This means regardless of what happens or the things that may trouble you in life you will still have peace.

This peace refers to a, "joining together in wholeness," and it indicates that you are not complete until you have connected yourself to the Spirit. Because the Spirit is what will allow you to deal with the people who have left you, betrayed you, even those that have beaten and bruised you physically. It not only strengthens you to move on in power (as Jesus did) but also forgive in the true Spirit of love and sincerity.

If we do not die to the flesh, or the desire to get even and get over on those that have harmed us, then we will respond to this hurt with the flesh. This is to respond in vengeance and with pain. If we continue to respond like this, we will continue to be hurt, and we will hurt others. It is a vicious cycle of hurt, and the only way to avoid it is to die to the flesh. As I continue to read and study the cross, I must admit that I don't know how Jesus dealt with the pain and suffering of such proportions, but it became practical that He died, indicating that we must also die to the flesh. We do this in our submission to the Spirit and the setting of our minds on the things of the Spirit. This may in most cases be best demonstrated by just exhibiting the fruit of the spirit (Galatians 5:22-23) in comparison to the works of the flesh (Galatians 5:19-21). In this way, you are alive to the Spirit.

We see this when the puncturing of His side brought forth blood and water but also forgiveness. I've heard many theological explanations for this, but there are only a few things that come from dying to the flesh and self. These are redemption and being Spirit led. These are the immediate reactions a person who puts their own selfish desires and those of the flesh to the side for the sake of being Christ-like. Their only fruit can be salvation and a life of the Spirit. Forgiveness, likewise, comes from God and being open to his Spirit. It is something only God can teach and those who are Spirit-filled will express.

To deal with people-inflicted pain, not only must we die to the flesh, but we must also be covered in the blood. This is as the Apostle put it, to be crucified with him, that the body of sin might be destroyed, that we should no longer serve sin. For he that is dead is freed from sin. Now if we are dead with Christ, we believe that this will also allow us life with Christ (Romans 6:6-11). Notice that He was covered in blood so we could be covered by blood. We are crucified "with" Christ. Our redemption is in His blood. So it is through Christ that we will forgive those who trespass against us.

By "blood" I am referring to the act in which He completed on Calvary. This is the same act that allows him to forgive us and also for us to forgive others. Through this we not only have the power of life but also the power to express a life of Christ to others. This is the power not only to forgive but also the power to extend mercy where it maybe needed. It is through this power and work in forgiveness that we are empowered to forgive even when it hurts.

I have had the pleasure of experiencing this very forgiveness and this Spirit-led reconciliation. If you have ever done a person wrong or did anything to hurt a person and are truly repentant and they respond in forgiveness, you can almost feel the presence of God. It is definitely evidence that the person who forgave is not just fleshly but an alive, loving, Spirit-filled person acting through their own sense of redemption and Spirit-led life because this is not something the Devil or the world will teach you.

These are great gifts that God has given us: forgiveness and redemption through blood. These are things in which the devil can't teach but also cannot steal. He can teach us to hate and seek revenge; he can take our cars, our houses, and our money, but the blood used to write our names in the Book of Life through Christ's sacrifice possesses such a power that the adversary simply cannot touch it.

YOUR CHALLENGE FOR DAY 8

Once we are covered in blood, dead to the flesh, we must be arrested by the Spirit. How many of us live a life so connected with God that we sweat and bleed Spirit? We will live and die for everything else, but seldom for the Spirit. We bleed gossip, we bleed backstabbing, and we bleed judgment of others, but not Spirit. Your challenge today is to let the Spirit arrest you now and every day, that you may be able to deal with what has been done to you and what will be done to you.

DAY 9

A Message for My Enemies

DAILY READING:
Romans 12:9-10, Proverbs 18:24, Psalm 23:5

And he saith unto them, "Be not affrighted: Ye seek Jesus of Nazareth, which was crucified: He is risen; He is not here: behold the place where they laid Him.
—MARK 16:6

EVER SINCE JESUS LEFT THE tomb, there have been some haters who stand in blatant opposition toward His followers. They come in all shapes and sizes, and they have one goal in mind: to deter our plans. Whether they are big or small, good looking or not so good looking, they are deterrents. They strive to keep us confined, away from an ever-present God in our lives. They are used for this purpose: as an attack on our spirituality, whether they are aware of it or not.

If we fight for ourselves and do not allow God to handle things, that thirst for revenge can become a wedge between us and God. The desire to cause another to fall will negatively affect your closeness to God. Scripture teaches us that we cannot offer anything to God if our brother has an ought with us (Matthew 5:23-24). How then, can we have an effective relationship with God if we harbor a hunger for revenge against our brother? How can we offer Him any praise in church if we hate the person sharing our pew or the people who live in our home? This also extends to those that we work with and even those that we serve with in ministry. In spite of what someone has done against us, we can allow God to avenge us, for this is doing right in His sight. Doing right may not always be easy, but this is the type of life that we have signed up for as believers and followers of Christ. If not, we will be just as guilty of sin as our hater and consequently experience his same fate which is eternal separation from God. We will both be enemies of God because of the issue or problem we have with one another.

The good news is that God has a message even for our haters. Just when they think they have confined us, just when they believe they have succeeded in the burial of a believer, God will leave behind a witness to testify just how good we are doing, just how far He has brought us, and just how blessed we really are in spite of their evil efforts.

Someone will be put in place just when our haters believe they have caught us, and that person will say, "He is not here!" They presume us to be nobodies, nothing of any substance or importance, but we're not across the train tracks with that impoverished, defeated mindset. Even if we are without money and rubbing our dimes together, we are not on the streets doing whatever is necessary to get one over on someone; plotting and scheming to make it. Most importantly, you yet belong to God and have not be overtaken by this world! We are not where they have been trying to put us! No, we are where God wants us to be, whether the haters like it or not. God has placed us here so that we are not only a living testimony of his goodness, but also to let the Devil and everyone else that doubted us know that, we are more than conquerors through Jesus who loved us (Romans 8:37). It is His love that gives us the will to go on, the will to be fruitful and prosperous.

Your Challenge for Day 9

Your challenge for today is to let God speak for you in opposition and in trial. Notice that when the opportunity was given for Jesus to speak His mind, He didn't utter a mumbling word. Rather, He allowed God to speak to His enemies through His victory over their attempt at confining Him. Jesus then allowed God to leave a witness behind of how good He was doing and how blessed He was. There will be a witness, so don't let the enemy—or the haters who work for him—cause you to backslide or lose your integrity. It will not be easy but in being risen with Christ, we must also rise above all opposing forces and attempts to keep you confined and unproductive.

DAY 10

Wise Counsel

DAILY READING:
Hebrews 4:14-16; 11:6, Psalm 121:1, Galatians 6:7-9, II Chronicles 7:14

*Blessed is the man who does not walk in the counsel of the wicked or
stand in the way of sinners or sit in the seat of mockers. But his delight
is in the law of the LORD, and on His law he meditates day and night.
He is like a tree planted by streams of water, which yields its fruit in
season and whose leaf does not wither. Whatever he does prospers.
Not so the wicked! They are like chaff that the wind blows away.*
— PSALM 1:1-4

THIS LESSON IS FOR THE individual who is his or her own problem.
Sometimes it is where we walk, stand and sit that causes to miss
out on a blessed life. Through methods of justification we have blamed
our upbringing, our misfortune and even the Devil, but we must face
the facts: sometimes, ***we are the problem***. Although our God is a God
of turnarounds, remember that U-turns start with "U!" I believe God! I
believe He can do what no other power can do, but I also know that God
does not bless those who work against Him. These can be the person or
persons who are in complete opposition of his plan, thus the Psalmist

declares, "The ungodly are not so" (Psalm 1:4). Or it can be those that really love God but do things contrary to his will and plan for their lives. For example, He has the power to deliver a person from HIV/AIDS, but will that person choose to give up the lifestyle that brought the virus on them in the first place? He has the power to place a person in a happy marriage, but can that person fix his or her attitude so their spouse can deal with them?

When I meet people who are disappointed or facing hardship, especially when they feel God has not moved when He should have, I have to ask, "Are you waiting on God, or is God waiting on you?" We have to understand that He is still "a rewarder of those who diligently seek Him" (Hebrews 11:6). So, while it is up to us to make the choice to change, He is the One we must turn to for our turnaround. This means that my destiny and the direction in which my life goes is often times based on where my relationship is with God my Maker. Sometimes my life is not where I would like it to be simply because I have failed to be the image of what God intended for me. I have not lived up to the potential in which God destined me to live up to which allows me to live beneath my potential.

God is the only one who possesses the power to change the unchangeable, to open doors that seem indefinitely closed. We need to consider the hills from which our help comes and understand that "all our help cometh from the Lord" (Psalm 121:1). He sits in Eternity with exactly what we need, holding our destiny and everything He promised to us in His hands.

Now, He is just waiting on us to make a move! This can be a move towards him or move out of His way so that He can work for you. It is God's intention at times to not just bless you but bless you according to the abilities and power he has already placed in you (Ephesians 3:20). Too often we make things so difficult when all God is asking is that we do our part.

I am not suggesting that we do something just for the sake of doing it, for there are many wrong things that can be done and are done. Rather, we should strive to do whatever falls within the will of God, and we can only do that if we have fervently and carefully sought to discover His will. Do something that connects with the heart of God and watch how the anxiety and stress of your predicament fades away. Your results maybe immediate or they may take a while but remember God is a rewarder of those who "diligently" seek him. This is not to make one attempt but to go after God as a hunter without food or water hunts as his only means of survival for the day. You survival is based on your connection with your Maker, and watch what God turns around for us when we turn around for Him. He is faithful and committed to those who are committed and faithful to Him.

"Doing our part" refers not only to where we walk, sit, and stand, nor does it only refer to the people with which we do these things It is also in reference to the way we think and our dependency on God. Sometimes we think to ourselves that God is not in control so we turn to other sources. God is still in control so our thinking and our pursuit of Him must be one that reflects that we believe He is still in control. We must be also willing to change some of the things we take pleasure in and find our delights. The Bible says of the God-following man, "His delight is in the law of the Lord, and in that law must he meditate both day and night" (Psalm 1:2).

After this comes the turnaround: " ...and he shall be like tree planted by the rivers of water, which bringeth forth his fruit in his season, and leaf also shall not wither, and whatsoever he doeth shall prosper" (Psalm 1:3). Notice how God never changes his position. Once you change your position with him, everything else falls into play.

YOUR CHALLENGE FOR DAY 10

Your challenge today is to do your part and to change some of your delights. This means that you might have to give up a "guilty pleasure" or be the bigger person in a situation that demands vengeance. We do this in order to by holy and acceptable before God. If you have spent any length of time in prayer or meditation of God and his Word, you will discover something that He is requiring of you. It may be the struggle but it's a struggle so God can get glory from your life.

DAY 11

We Are What We Eat

DAILY READING:
I John 2:26-27, Romans 8:14-15, Isaiah 63:10

On the last and greatest day of the feast, Jesus stood and said in a loud voice,
"If anyone is thirsty, let him come to me and drink. Whoever believes in me,
as the scripture has said, streams of living water will flow from within him."
—JOHN 7:37-38

JESUS WAS TALKING ABOUT THE believer in this text, but it is a two-sided coin. Whether we are saved or unsaved, we all have a core—something inside of us that is bound to come out. By core I am referring to the soul of a man: the seat of his emotions, intellect and will. "What is fed to the soul will prove what is leading the soul." If it is fed by the Spirit, then it will follow after Christ. On the other hand, if it is fed by the flesh, it will follow after the flesh. Thus, "We are what we eat."

We all have a desire to do certain things, but those who thirst for Christ and drink of Him will exhibit Christ outwardly. Whether we want to admit it or not, what is inside of us will eventually find its way to the surface If we are unwilling to let go of things that feed negative behavior such as lust, anger, and bitterness than it will remain and grow within the soul of a man.

As Christians, it is not our goal to be carnal, nor soulish (2 Timothy 1:13), but spiritual. This can only come through what you feed yourself.

I must recommend that daily meditation on scripture along with some fasting and prayer will help you grow in the Spirit. These are activities that not only build a self denial for things and activities that will feed your flesh but they also awaken the Spirit man and your connection with God. Jesus told his disciples that they were to fast and pray until he returned (Matthew 9:14-15), so we should be committed to these same spiritual disciplines.

As many women know all too well, the way to a man's heart is often through his stomach. In this same way, Jesus can reach your core, because that is where your soul and Spirit live. If Jesus can get into your core, then you will be spiritually productive. He said in John 7:38, "out of his belly will flow streams of living water." This is in reference to a "womb" or our "inner man," which tells us that our spirit should be productive. It is Jesus that will help you give birth or produce something that is worth keeping.

Notice that Jesus got up on the last day of the feast. They had eaten and should be full but something was still missing from them. This is how we are in America. We are a gluttonous nation that will eat and eat and chase after things that are temporarily pleasing. Often, we have tried everything worth trying and are still left unsatisfied. We have a drink of everything else on the table, yet we still feel thirsty. Similarly, after we have exhausted all our options, we are still empty somehow.

We can never make enough love to be happy, drink enough alcohol to be satisfied, nor eat enough food to be full. In fact, if we eat enough of the wrong stuff, we'll suffer aches and pains. Being full of the Spirit, on the other hand, will never cause any harm. Far too many of us are very full of many things but remain spiritually malnourished.

We are often guilty of giving lip service to Jesus, claiming that we love Him and live for Him but failing when push comes to shove. Jesus says that if we drink of Him, we will earn the right to be called His (John 6:53-56). This position of Sonship is only obtained by being Spirit led. Thus, I urge you today to feed yourself Christ so that your Spirit is good and productive. It is then, and only then, can we produce something worth saving and worth keeping around. To be Spirit led will give you all those things that make life worth living. It produces life and peace for you (Romans 8:6).

Some of us have aborted what we were producing for Christ by rejecting Him or feeding our selfish desires. There is no condemnation to them that are in Christ, who walk not after the flesh but the Spirit (Romans 8:1). These are both necessary to be spiritually healthy. You must accept Christ into your life and walk after his Spirit because without them abortion or termination of your purpose is inevitable. Without this acceptance and a spirit-led life what we produce is already dead: dead dreams, dead plans, and dead visions that are not Christ centered but are self-centered. We get out what we put in, and if we consume garbage, we will inevitably produce something not worthy of living.

Some of us have some unrealized dreams lodged in our bellies, some misguided potential in our stomachs that will never come to fruition. We consume things that lower our self-esteem and self-awareness, and this destroys our capability to accomplish the goals that live within us.

If we have the Spirit, we should bear His fruit or His characteristics which are: love, joy, peace, long-suffering, gentleness, goodness, faith, meekness, and temperance (Galatians 5:22). We need to fill our cups with enough Christ that our core overflows with the Spirit.

YOUR CHALLENGE FOR DAY 11

Your challenge today is to be filled with the Spirit. Do not allow anything to spoon-feed you other than God. Otherwise, like a stray dog starving for love and affection, you might find yourself obeying the bell of a master who does not love you. The worst situation to be in is to serve something or someone who does not love you, for a self-serving master like that will feed you unhealthy things with no regard to whether you survive or not.

DAY 12

What's Flowing from Our Bellies?

DAILY READING:
Joel 2:28, Galatians 6:7-9, Galatians 5:19-22

On the last and greatest day of the feast, Jesus stood and said in a loud voice,
"If anyone is thirsty, let him come to me and drink. Whoever believes in me,
as the scripture has said, streams of living water will flow from within him."
—JOHN 7:37-38

THE BIBLE TELLS US, " ...IN the last days, He will pour out His Spirit upon all flesh" (Joel 2:28). This is partially because, in the last days, people are looking for evidence and an effective witness—not only those who speak, but also those who actually walk upright before them. In a sense, we must live what we pump out. We can no longer speak truth while living lies; we must be an example and lead people in the right direction.

God had to pour something on this flesh. We dress up and camouflage ourselves in our Sunday best, but the flesh is still revealed still doing too much in our place of sacredness. He decided He would clothe us in His Spirit. He had to pour something on us that we might be pleasing to Him—something capable of burying the flesh or humanity.

Thus, we must be careful about what we allow to reside in our bellies or our inner man. Much like if you want a healthy body you must become more disciplined in both exercise and what you eat, we too must be careful about what we consume or take in. We also must not lack in those spiritual disciplines such as prayer, fasting and a good devotional life.

If we are going to be what God is spiritually calling us to be, we definitely must examine ourselves daily and be aware of what we consume. This is to enforce some definite dietary restrictions. For example, Hannah of the Old Testament, who was a barren woman was found praying with the bitterness of soul. God eventually blessed her with a son in whom we know to be Samuel. But when Eli looked on her, he observed her lips are moving but her voice is not heard. He even thought her to be drunk. My point is that when bitterness is in the soul, it will come from your lips.

Hear this Saints! You ought to be careful about what you consume because it will affect you significantly. It will affect your health, your prayer life, and even your love life. It was Hannah's bitterness that not only kept her from having a son but also her husband. These are detrimental to the soul and your person because they will come out of you. Hannah also shows us that God has enough mercy to answer prayer in spite of our attitude or disposition.

The Apostle Paul described a bitter and jealous person as "unprofitable." He writes, "they are all gone out of the way, they are together become unprofitable; there is none that doeth good, no, not one. Their throat is an open sepulcher; with their tongues they have used deceit; the poison of asps is under their lips: whose mouth is full of cursing and bitterness: their feet are swift to shed blood: Destruction and misery are their ways: And the way of peace they have not known." (Romans 3:12-17)

This is the person you can become if you are not careful about what you consume. You will go to sleep one way and wake up this kind of person. Not because life was so hard on you or that God had turned his back on you, but because of what you decided to feed yourself.

Prayerfully, we understand now that depression and anxiety and things of this sort are detrimental to our soul. Jealousy and envy will eat you from the inside out, and your works will be the works of these rather than the works of God. When these "unholy emotions" live in you, they reside in the soul of a person. Sometimes God puts us into situations that require us to survive off of something inward, so we must be certain that what exists within us is of God. Otherwise we will respond to hardships and deal with matters through carnal perspectives rather than the Spirit of God.

There is deliverance that resides in each of us. Our survival will sometimes be based on our inward man. For example, it is from our spirits that we muster up the strength to press on or progress forward. Let me say again: God sometimes wants to bless you with the abilities and power he has already given you (Ephesians 3:20).

There are many biblical examples of something inward blessing people who were in bad situations. For example, Moses saved his mother from the enslavement of the Pharaoh. Jesus saved His mother from the bondage of sin. Eve gave birth to a son, and she was excited because she was sure what was within her was something that would "bruise the serpent's head" (Genesis 3:15). But instead, she gave birth to Cain, who ultimately murdered his brother Abel, all out of jealousy. This tells me that while there is deliverance within us, we are also capable of birthing something that will kill or destroy whatever is nearest and dearest to us, such as God's plan for our lives, our dreams, and our visions for the future.

YOUR CHALLENGE FOR DAY 12

The challenge for you today is not to try and bring God down to human levels. Instead, you must allow Him to reign divine. The goal is for humans to live Spirit-filled lives. Although the Spirit does help us in our infirmities, He is just a help. I encourage you today to make a conscious decision to do better and to be better for the One who saved us and a world that needs us.

DAY 13

Why Pay to Go to Hell When You Can Go for Free?

DAILY READING:
Matthew 3:2, Luke 5:32; 13:5; 15:7, Revelations 3:19

*And he cast down the pieces of silver in the temple
and departed and went and hanged himself.*
—MATTHEW 27:5

*L*IKE IT OR NOT, SOMEWHERE down the line, at one time or another, we all have to express a sincere apology for mistakes we have made. Mothers and fathers have had to repent or apologize to their children because of how they raised them or for being absent from the picture altogether. Brothers and siblings have had to apologize through the years for the competitiveness and envy they have held against one another. If this is true in human relationships, how can we have a proper relationship with God unless we are willing to repent? This is something we should be asking ourselves, especially since we are the ones who will inevitably make all the mistakes.

In our relationship with God, failure to repent results in the death of that relationship. This failure to admit where we went wrong can harm our relationship with God. Because in repentance we not only ask God for his forgiveness but we also in a sense forgive ourselves. We do this in the acknowledging of our wrongdoing and the turning from it. If it is a besetting sin or one of those in which you are having difficulty totally giving up, I would advise you to again retreat to a place of quietness and seclusion with God with fasting and prayer to finally get things right between you and God. If the truth be told, God wants to forgive you more than you want to repent. I have discovered that in fasting I am not only disciplining myself in what not to eat or not eating at all, but my total person becomes more disciplined even in the areas in which I am having difficulty showing discipline.

You may call a fast for yourself and go into a season of prayer for something like alcohol abuse or pill addiction but even in that, you discipline yourself to spend money better or refraining from shopping as much.

This was not the case for Judas Iscariot. I am not suggesting that Judas did not feel any regret or remorse for what he had done, but regret is not the same as repentance. Guilt should not be the object of our repentance; rather, our aim should be a sincere turnaround and change. I have not included many devotions on repentance here because it is something we are all aware of but we tend to avoid. However, I purposely include plenty of scripture for the believer who does not see the use of repentance. The church will wrong God and be at odds with Him, then show up on Sunday morning to give Him glory, honor, and praise. This becomes a sad indictment of the people who will not admit fault to the One who presents them faultless before His presence. By this I mean that if God is going to present you faultless or free from wrongdoing because you honestly confess, I think our best option is to simply turn to him in repentance.

Notice that Judas did give his portion of the money back to his accomplices, but he did not give God his heart. Some of us tend to admit fault when guilt finally gets the best of us, but we will not admit our offenses to God. We must admit our sin, without self-justification, and we must plead for His mercy. Judas did not do this; he simply turned himself over to the adversary in suicide—the dead sacrifice that Satan requires. Thus, Jesus does not declare him as one of his (John 17:12). C.S Lewis explains that God loves and respects your baby steps. In spite of our call to perfection and holiness, like any father, he is proud of the child who attempts his first walk even though they may stumble. He is not proud of the fall but the attempt to be right before him. Thus, repentance is daily practice that we all must commit ourselves.

God will honor your attempt to make things right with him. Lewis also suggest, that God is easy to please but hard to satisfy. However, we have the opportunity through Christ to turn from our wicked ways and seek His face. Then, we have the ability to present ourselves a living sacrifice, holy and acceptable unto God. This is again that, "reasonable service" that I talked about in Day One.

YOUR CHALLENGE FOR DAY 13

Repentance is that true, genuine turning to God and admitting fault, while pleading for his help through Jesus Christ to help you change your ways. He will do this for no other motive than your love for God and your sincerest apology for how you have wrong him. A heartfelt sorry leads to a heartfelt change. This is the beginning of a good relationship with God. Scripture teaches, "If we confess our sins, He is faithful and just to forgive us our sins and cleanse us from all unrighteousness. If we say we have not sinned, we make Him a liar, and His Word is not in us" (I John 1:9). Our challenge today is to commit to a turnaround, to rid ourselves daily of things that are displeasing to God, and to make our offenses known to Him in the sincerest of apologies. This can be done through prayer and fasting but will also take time, discipline, and some positive energy with a positive attitude. So I urge you today, turn your heart and repent.

DAY 14

The Heavy-Handed Grip of God

DAILY READING:
John 15:12-17, II Timothy 4:5, Philippians 3:8

*The hand of the LORD was upon me, and He brought
me out by the Spirit of the LORD and set me down in
the middle of the valley; and it was full of bones.*
—EZEKIEL 37:1

I AM GLAD THE HAND OF the Lord is upon me, because it distinguishes me from those who do not reside with Him. I have found that when we are touched by forbidden hands, they have a tendency to taint us. This is the reason we do not have more than one wife or husband, for it may ruin us to be touched by another. By this I mean it will taint our purity because we have been separated for our spouses and God alone in this manner. For this reason, infections and STDs exist. This is why even in ministry we are not hasty to lay on hands, for it may negatively affect our purity (I Timothy 5:22). And the servant of God must be pure!

Let us not forget that we are called to purity, even though we are susceptible to fall. Thus, we are in a battle, because living in the Spirit will set us up to be a target of the enemy and even our own flesh. The flesh is in opposition against God, and I believe that it can feel God's hand on us and the Spirit active in our life. The flesh is constantly leading us to do things that please only us and displease God. The problem lies in that God's hand is on us. He's reaching us from Eternity, and we are yet in the natural, subject to whatever life may bring us.

Therefore, it becomes the powerful, loving grip of God that keeps us focused and grounded in Him. Although he does not take our free will, the hand of the Lord reminds us that we are called to his service and his will. It will even make you uncomfortable when you are doing things contrary to what He has called you. Sometimes, because He is God, His seemingly heavy-handed grip can cause us some God-inflicted pain. His grip is so tight, but his Spirit is so gentle. These are both necessary to mature the believer into purpose as it is always better for a child to have both parents. Thus, the Spirit of God and the grip of God work together in our growth.

A paradox, a contradiction of sorts exists: The hand of the Lord was upon me, which can indicate some pressure or some work, but "His Spirit has brought me out."

Sometimes God puts His powerful hands on us to do just that: to bring us out or pull us through. I'm reminded of when Jesus threw the merchants out of the temple (Matthew 21:12). This was a natural beating, but in some instances, some Jewish-thinking believers may have been beaten out of the temple because God was starting a church.

In an effort to disconnect us from that we are so tightly connected to, God's grip may cause some pain. He often times uses pain to remove us from all the temporal and fickle pleasures and false hope we have put in ourselves and in other people and things. He wants us to put our hope in Him, because he is worthy of that.

My issue with God, however, is not His heavy-handed grip or His gentle Spirit. He effectively governs our humanity with His heavenly genius. This is seen when He asked Ezekiel to prophesy about his bad situation. My issue is that I can be in conflict but God still wants me to do ministry. Ezekiel is experienced a bringing out in his personal life but he was not granted a break or a vacation. God wanted him to be spiritual and commit to a spiritual work. I know it is hard to be spiritual and suffer at the same time, and it is even harder to suffer and minister to others. But ministry becomes so much more effective when it is on the other side of a test and you have been victorious.

I thought it was a great inconvenience to be called to minister while you suffer personally but then you realize that your calling and ministry is not about yourself but those in which I minister. Ministry and suffering are connected. Paul used his suffering to prove his ability in ministry (2 Corinthians 11:23-33). I know God sits high and looks low, but when I'm in the middle of a crisis, I wonder how God expects me to be spiritual? When I just want to give up and throw in the towel, I am still expected to love my enemies and keep a constant prayer line between me and God. He then becomes our Counselor, one whom we can cast our cares upon and he will keep us.(Psalm 55:22).

Like you, I am often attacked by things that touch me, things I am experiencing in the here and now. When this happens, God wants us to use the abilities and gifts He's given us to handle it all. Perhaps He wants us to use some ability that we have underestimated the power or priority of, something that seems unaffiliated with the problem. One way we can do this is to speak life into those dead situations, to talk better even when things are not better. This is to embrace the power that is in your tongue (Proverbs 8:21). We will often times, speak death more than life, pain more than promises; and this is where our downfall often begins.

If we do things in the Spirit or those things that are faith-based in Jesus Christ, then the Spirit will reach into our personal situations and carry us through. I know this to be true as I have worked for employers that could not stand the Spirit that resided in me. They had no reason to dislike me or purpose in their hearts to work against me but they did and as soon as I responded in faith, the Lord delivered me. Whether it was to better job or a better location, God is a deliverer if your put your trust in Him.

That same Spirit brought Ezekiel out from somewhere, and it must have been some kind of horrible place if Ezekiel considered the Valley of

Bones to be an upgrade and a blessing. The Bible says the Lord brought him out and set him in the place of bones. We are not given the place in which God brought him from but if he was brought out by the Lord and set in the valley of bones it was a place worse than the valley. God will not deliver you from something to place you into an even worse situation.

In our humanity we may be delivered by God and go into a worse situation but he delivers us for a better outcome. Sometimes, God upgrades the person and not the circumstances. Maybe the valley was not better but Ezekiel was better because of where God had brought him from.

Sometimes God will bring you from a place of testing to put you in another trying situation, not to change your circumstance but to change you. This was likely true in Ezekiel's case, just as it often is in ours. We need to learn to have such a closeness with our God that we can ask him, "What are you trying to teach me now?"

He might just change *you* instead of your situation. Sometimes God will change us so we will make an effort to change our circumstances. Why? Because some of us are so stubborn that if God didn't change us, we would remain stuck in our brokenness. I know God's hand is on me, changing me so I can change my situation. Because if I keep changing sceneries then I become a rolling stone, or an unstable person so God changes me to deal with whatever situation I find myself in.

Your Challenge for Day 14

Your challenge today is to let God begin the process of shaping and molding you into who He would have you to be. Do the work He has called you to do and do it until there is fruition. Do not forsake humble beginnings. Do not quit just because you think you have no support. Simply carry out this burden until it is a blessing.

DAY 15

Are You Waiting on God, or Is God Waiting on You?

DAILY READING:
Psalms 37; 27:14; 37:9

Hast thou not known, hast thou not heard, that the everlasting God, the LORD, the Creator of the ends of the Earth, fainteth not, neither is weary? There is no searching of His understanding. He giveth power to the faint; and to them that have no might, He increaseth strength. Even the youths shall faint and be weary, and the young men shall utterly fall: But they that wait upon the LORD shall renew their strength; they shall mount up with wings as eagles; they shall run, and not be weary; and they shall walk, and not faint.
—ISAIAH 40:28-31

IN A REAL LOVE AFFAIR, there are some things that are worth the wait. There are things we should not experience too early, or we will destroy the sanctity of the covenant. Lovers can wait, if they really love you. I waited three long years for another chance with the love of my life. Five if you include the years I waited in distance from here as she was a state away. Ten years (we are high school sweet hearts) if you include the time I had to wait before God had perfected us and I could marry her. But with God, we should never assume that he is the slothful one or the one playing hard to get. There comes a time when we should ask, "Am I waiting on Him, or is He waiting on me?"

We can never really know whether God is waiting on us or we on Him unless we become fruit inspectors. By this I mean we must become aware of the state we are in to see if God is waiting on us. For example, those who are waiting on God, know that He will give power to the faint, He will increase the strength of those with no might, and He will renew our strength. So if you are waiting on Him to perform something that He promised, you may get weak and even weary but there will be a renewing in His timing. Also, when we wait on Him, we will mount up with wings as eagles, we will run and not be weary, and we will walk and not faint (Isaiah 40:31).

On the other hand, if He is waiting on us, He does not get weary or worn out. He waits in eternity, he never sleeps nor slumbers (Psalm 121:4). His position never changes. He will still be sitting high and looking low while we wait in natural time and are affected by our own slothfulness. If God is waiting on us, we will be anxious, warring in our mind. We will experience some sleepless nights because of the stress of our situations. We will have a need to quit or retire in our Spirit. But either way, we must not be weary in doing good, "for in due season, [we] will reap if [we] faint not" (Galatians 6:9).

YOUR CHALLENGE FOR DAY 15

If God is waiting on you, make an effort to seek Him out and discover what He is waiting for you to do. Where have you exhibited delayed obedience? Where has your relationship declined in degree of intimacy? You must ignite that fire with God, that longing to do His will. If He is waiting on you, then you have some renewed strength coming your way; God does not make promises He will not keep.

If you are waiting on God, your challenge today is to just keep doing what you are doing. Keep up the good work and do not grow weary. Remember that He never sleeps nor slumbers (Psalms 121:4). He is always working and blessing, though always in His time. Be mindful: He is sitting in eternity while we catch up with him. Think of it this way: you are not really waiting on Him, but *on* time to catch up with God's eternal plan. Because you are doing the will of God, you can embrace Psalm 37 today: "Fret not thyself because of evildoers, neither be thou envious against the workers of iniquity. For they shall soon be cut down like the grass and wither as the green herb. Trust in the Lord, and do good; so shalt thou dwell in the land, and verily thou shalt be fed. Delight thyself in the Lord; and He shall give thee the desires of thine heart. Commit thy way unto the Lord; trust also in Him; and He shall bring it to pass" (Psalm 37:1-5).

DAY 16

What a Friend We Have in Jesus

DAILY READING:
Romans 5:6-10, Proverbs 18:24, Isaiah 41:8, I Timothy 2:5

Henceforth I call you not servants; for the servant knoweth not what his lord doeth: but I have called you friends; for all things that I have heard of my Father I have made known unto you. Ye have not chosen me, but I have chosen you and ordained you, that ye should go and bring forth fruit, and that your fruit should remain: that whatsoever ye shall ask of the Father in my name, He may give it you. These things I command you, that ye love one another. If the world hate you, ye know that it hated me before it hated you. If ye were of the world, the world would love his own: but because ye are not of the world, but I have chosen you out of the world, therefore the world hateth you.
—JOHN 15:15-19

ODAY, WE DISCOVER THE HATRED of the world for our Savior and even for us. Thus, we must learn to deal with hatred and haters. As long as we live on this Earth, we will be hated. If we are not hated, we must check whose side we are on! In fact, anything or anyone that is against God is an enemy of ours because anything against God will be against the

God that lives within us. We can even safely assume that the very flesh in which we are dressed goes against God, so we need to pay close attention to all of our carnal desires, lest we become enemies of God ourselves.

The world seems to have an ongoing love and leave relationship with God in which He loves them, yet they are still on a mission to remove Him. We, too, would have continued in this way had it not been for Jesus. We would be against Him, striving to help the world with His removal rather than helping Him to spread the truth of His gospel. Because of Jesus, we are on the right side, working for a godly cause. He bought us with a price and saved us from ourselves.

The interesting thing is that even though He owns us, He does not make us slaves. Instead, He allows us to be co-owners of ourselves, and He considers us friends. If we be counted as a friend of God, then we are trusted not to betray or backstab Him. This includes denying Him, acting as though we are not His whenever we are in the presence of sinners. If we do not let our light shine wherever we go, regardless of the circumstances or who is around us, we are guilty of not being a good friend of God. Everyone who meets us should be able to tell that we are connected to Him. If we are co-owners of ourselves and Jesus bought us with a price, then we should check with Him before we do things. Everything we do should be with His permission and His blessing. Nevertheless, He is such a friend that He still loves us and cares for us, even when we go to certain places and do ungodly things.

This is the whole idea of being Spirit led and directed by God. This is to have your steps ordered by His perfect will or His plan for your life. We are to be His disciples, not disciples of one another. We follow Christ and submit to his authority and leadership. When we are disciples of God, we do as the Master has taught us by His own example and our lives will be bonded with His through the denying of ourselves(Matthew16:24).

If we become disciples of one another, we will all lead one another to backslide; truly a case of the blind leading the blind, for we are all blind without His sight. I know this to be true because, I have been unsaved and have ministered to the unsaved. I have discovered that the gospel is hidden to them (2 Corinthians 4:3). They are blinded by the things of this world, unable to learn spiritual things. Self-denial is something that is spiritual. It is only done by those who can see through Jesus Christ that they are not human beings doing spiritual acts but rather spiritual beings trapped in humanity and the world, and all that is whether it began in the mouth of God spoken in the case of light (Genesis 1:3) or breathed in the case of life (Genesis 2:7).

He is a great friend to have, for there are things that are impossible with our earthly friends. No matter how hard they try, no matter how good they may be, there will inevitably come a time when our friends will fail or betray us because they are human. God, on the other hand, will never fail us, and He can do what others cannot. He is God, and as such He has all rights and privileges. Yet, he is also friend enough to give us second, third, fourth and fifth chances. He is God enough to call us to a turnaround, but He is friend enough to warn us of the mistakes we are about to make. He is God enough to judge us according to our works, but He is also friend enough to anoint us with His Son's precious blood and snatch me from a world that not only hates Him, but one that is also destined for Hell.

YOUR CHALLENGE FOR DAY 16

Your challenge today is to avoid taking your friendship with God for granted. If He is willing to be a friend that "sticketh closer than a brother," we must not sell Him out for the sake of impressing the world. Be a friend of God, for He is both a friend and a God to you. Our task is to not allow worldly influences to remove Him from His rightful position in our lives.

DAY 17

Forgiving When It Hurts

DAILY READING:
Matthew 6:12, 14; 18:21-35, Luke 6:37

Then said Jesus, "Father, forgive them; for they know not what they do." And they parted His raiment, and cast lots.
—LUKE 23:34

JESUS FORGAVE US EVEN WHEN it hurt. Too many of us justify our unforgiveness by how much pain or suffering we endure, when we should consider it as the opportune time to forgive. Open wounds and bruised flesh do not justify unforgiveness. After all, Christ forgave us while he was bearing the pain of fresh wounds and bruises filled with nails—injuries and undeserved punishments caused by His children, people who claimed to be His friends. To forgive as Christ forgave, we must put some real blood on our forgiveness.

Even with thorns poking into the flesh of His guiltless head, He had enough sense, enough compassion to forgive. We, on the other hand, push forgiveness aside because the stress of the situation causes us a migraine. How many of us can be honest and say we have flipped out on someone because of a migraine or a stress headache? How many times have you just simply lost it on the guilty, the innocent, and the untried, all because of a pain in our heads that was caused or not caused by them? Yet Jesus forgives us all, even when we are the cause of His aches and pains.

We must forgive if we are to embrace this covenant we have with God. We must forgive others because He forgave us. He forgave us with a sacrifice of His blood, paid with His pain for the unrighteous things that bring us pleasure. Scripture even teaches us that those who will not forgive might miss Heaven (Matthew 18:34-35). Holding grudges and being stubborn will cause you to miss out on those streets of gold. Still, we act like forgiveness is some secondary notion that can be dismissed or overlooked because it is difficult for us. Even the disciples, human as they were, knew enough to avoid asking Jesus to "increase their faith" (Luke 17:5) until they had to forgive when it hurt. It was not until He said, "If he trespasses against thee seven times and repents, thou shalt forgive him" (Luke 17:4) that they asked for more faith.

But why is it so difficult to forgive someone for their trespasses? The answer is simple: When we forgive, we often do not see an immediate reward. Sometimes we may feel better about the situation or be released from the pain and bondage of holding a grudge, but unless we have truly forgiven sacrificially, we will still be unprofitable servants because we have only done what was required of us and nothing more.

YOUR CHALLENGE FOR DAY 17

Your challenge today is to forgive when it hurts. Forgive your betrayers, those who backstab and persecute you. Forgive those you loved and trusted, only to see them turn their back on you when you needed them most. Crawl out from under the tracks where they threw you and forgive them as Jesus would and does. Paul encourages us to forgive in the person of Christ, lest Satan should take advantage of us, for we are aware of his devices (II Corinthians 2:10-11).

Day 18

Changing Season

DAILY READING:
Philippians 3:8, Galatians 6:7-9

Man that is born of a woman is of few days, and full of trouble.
He cometh forth like a flower and is cut down: he fleeth also as a
shadow and continueth not … If a man die, shall he live again? All
the days of my appointed time will I wait, till my change come..
—JOB 14:1-2, 14

IF WE ARE DOING RIGHT and living right, there will come a time when the enemy will declare war on us. When the enemy does this he rolls up his sleeves and tries to push us back into whatever God has delivered us from. He will try and hit near and dear to our hearts so that our emotions will be involved. As painstaking as this process can be, our love for God must be tested. As with all relationships, the one we share with God will not grow or mature until the love has been tried or tested. Thus, while the devil is working against God, he is actually working for the maturity of the believer. This maturing must occur in order for us to find the intimacy we desire. We cannot stagnate and let our love for

God remain on the same level it was when we were first saved. We must continue to love Him more and more.

The beautiful thing about changing our game plan and playing on a different team is that it forces the devil to do what he has the most difficulty doing: find some new tricks. He must resort to new tactics because we will not fall for the same old traps. We are through fighting and crying over those same old issues. If the enemy can wave the same stimuli before us and we continue to fall for it, we are in need of spiritual growth.

When "changing season" comes, we mustn't be discouraged by the dramas of seasons past, by the mistakes of years gone by. I am not talking about seasons such as winter, summer, and spring, but about hunting season, when we are like the rabbit or deer, with the adversary hot on our trail. When we are making progress in our spiritual relationship with God, the enemy will consider it to be "believer season," and we will be relentlessly hunted down by him.

God allows this so that the devil in Hell cannot convince us that we have not changed or been delivered. This is the season in which we have the opportunity to prove to our haters that we are still God's children. This is changing season, the time when God can promote and will promote our growth if we will allow it.

This is not the time to die or be defeated; it is the season to excel and keep up the good things that we are doing and striving for. We can't throw in the towel on our marriages or our ministries! This is the season to reignite that fire and become a trailblazer for the God who ordained our present situation.

YOUR CHALLENGE FOR DAY 18

So what is your challenge today? You must make God proud that you have survived. In this season, continue in the direction you were headed, as long as it is a godly one. Do not abort any missions! Simply continue in the perfect will of God.

DAY 19

The ugly side of progress

Daily Reading:
I Corinthians 12:4-7; 12:11-12; 18; 24-27, Romans 17:9-10

*And when the LORD saw that Leah was hated, He opened her womb:
but Rachel was barren. And Leah conceived and bare a son, and she
called his name Reuben: for she said, "Surely the LORD hath looked
upon my affliction; now therefore my husband will love me." And she
conceived again, and bare a son; and said, "Because the LORD hath
heard I was hated, He hath therefore given me this son also": and she
called his name Simeon. And she conceived again, and bare a son;
and said, "Now this time will my husband be joined unto me, because
I have born him three sons": therefore was his name called Levi. And
she conceived again, and bare a son: and she said, "Now will I praise
the LORD": therefore, she called his name Judah; and left bearing.*
—GENESIS 29:31-35

I N THIS TEXT, WE SEE the other side of productivity. There is an, "ugly side to progress." We love the blossoming and the ripening of fruitfulness, but there is a side of these that we rarely like to consider: the time of cutting off.

Every good, fruitful, healthy piece of fruit, whether grape, apple, or otherwise, faces being cut from its vine by someone or something. This is a very dangerous situation for that fruit. From a spiritual standpoint, the vine sustains and matures us, and when we are cut off from it, not only are we headed toward the devil's Hell, but we may also be in danger of taking others with us to our doom.

While others may hate us, and while we may fear being cut off, we must continue in progress. It is important to realize that when pruning season comes, God will be doing the trimming and not man. We must be prepared to receive His pruning so that we might bear more fruit (John 15:2). God does this so that we might be more productive, but the enemy will cut at us simply because we are blessed. We are not hated because we have displeased God or because there is anything wrong or abnormal about us. Rather, we are hated because of the abnormality and insufficiency of our enemy.

YOUR CHALLENGE FOR DAY 19

Your challenge today is not to let anyone or anything disconnect you from God and from progress. The enemy desires to cut you off from life and ministry to prevent you from being a blessing to others. Be strong in the Lord and continue doing what you are doing unto the glory of God. Remember that you cannot quit because someone needs you!

DAY 20

You Don't Have to Be Preferred to Be Productive

DAILY READING:
Psalm 139:13-14, Philippians 4:13

*And when the LORD saw that Leah was hated, He opened her womb:
but Rachel was barren. And Leah conceived and bare a son, and she
called his name Reuben: for she said, "Surely the LORD hath looked
upon my affliction; now therefore my husband will love me." And she
conceived again, and bare a son; and said, "Because the LORD hath
heard I was hated, He hath therefore given me this son also": and she
called his name Simeon. And she conceived again, and bare a son;
and said, "Now this time will my husband be joined unto me, because
I have born him three sons": therefore was his name called Levi. And
she conceived again, and bare a son: and she said, "Now will I praise
the LORD": therefore, she called his name Judah; and left bearing.*
—GENESIS 29:31-35

I N THE BIBLE, LEAH WAS unattractive, yet she was fruitful. On the
contrary, her sister Rachel was very attractive, but she was barren.

Sometimes, the most productive things are not packaged as beautifully as others. Some things look good but don't last long. They may be impressive on the outside but empty and worthless and corroded beneath the immaculate surface.

We can take Rachel's barrenness as a firm warning: If we are not careful, God can and will shut down our operations. We must be careful what we say and do because God may cut us off if we try to do so to others. There are times in life when we will be hated, not only out of jealousy of our productivity, but also because we are not the preferred choice.

In the direction God leads us, they may not like our kind. Maybe they don't like our race, our gender, the way we speak, or even our hair color. No matter what others think, though, if God sends us, we absolutely must go! If He's leading us to do something, and if He is with us, we simply cannot fail.

It is a natural human condition to want to be accepted. Those who are not accepted suffer some frustration and embarrassment. But the reality is that no matter how many changes we make to impress others, we still may never be accepted. If we are not careful, our need to be accepted may enslave us to someone and their ideas of what we should be and what we should do—and in the end, we still may not be their preferred choice. Eventually, we must become comfortable in our own skin and go to our Creator and allow Him to help us master whoever it is that He wants us to be. Bishop T.D. Jakes says in his book, *Maximize the Moment: God's Action Plan for Your Life*, "there is a difference between having potential and performing to your potential."

Leah was not the preferred choice based on her physical appearance, but she was still able to perform to her potential. She represents the high school dropout, the teen mother, the ex-con, yet she fulfilled her purpose. Why? Because in God, we don't have to be preferred to be productive. We may have a lazy eye, a club foot, or some other noticeable abnormality, but it makes no difference. Leah was not the prettiest, but God opened her womb. God can open doors that no man can open. Despite the hate and the opposition she faced, Leah conceived. Despite her ailments and disabilities and inferiorities, she bore several sons. Regardless of those watching and laughing, God looked down on her in her affliction, blessed her, and allowed her to be used for His purposes. Despite the fact that man didn't want her, she conceived again and again. Absent of the father who sold her, she conceived, and—most importantly—after giving birth, she forgot all about her doubters and gave all praise to God!

Your Challenge for Day 20

Today, I challenge you to give praise to God, even if you are not the preferred choice, for you can still be productive in your ministry, marriage, and all your endeavors. This is a spiritual challenge as well as a social one. Because believers and the Church are both spiritual and social, we should be socially gifted as well as spiritually gifted. Today, I challenge you not only to recognize the beauty and the gifts in you, but also those in someone else. Remember that we are all part of God's body, each necessary in our own way

DAY 21

Is your heart in the right place?

DAILY READING:
II Chronicles 16:9, Philippians 4:8-9, Proverbs 3:5; 23:74

Blessed are the pure in heart: for they shall see God.
—MATTHEW 5:8

A PURE HEART IS THE BEGINNING of being sold out for God, because in a pure heart devoted to God, there is no competition for Him. When our hearts are impure, God is forced to compete for our attention and adoration, and we experience complications because of whatever it is that causes the impurity.

Some of our hearts are dislocated from God and His purpose. Thus, we experience complications in our lives. There will always be defect in our spiritual walk if we are trying to live for God under the constraints, emotions, and ideas of an old heart. The Bible tells us, "The eyes of the Lord run to and fro throughout the whole Earth, to shew Himself strong in behalf of them whose heart is perfect toward Him" (II Chronicles 16:9). The passage goes on to say, "Thou hast done foolishly; therefore from henceforth thou shalt have wars."

Bearing this warning in mind, could it be that we have missed God in what we are doing? Is this why we are immersed in fleshly battles, integrity wars, and spiritual stress? Who would have thought that our heart condition could cause such problems in our daily lives? As the passage clearly states, if we are suffering from a heart problem, we could very well be at war. The blessing here is that He does not war against us; instead, He turns us over to war against ourselves and others. Have you ever wondered why you have so many internal battles and mental conflicts? If this is something you are suffering from, my advice is to check your heart condition.

YOUR CHALLENGE FOR DAY 21

Your challenge today is to have a pure heart for God. This may not come easy, but think on pure things. Remember: Whatsoever you think in your heart, so will you be (Proverbs 23:7). This is one of the downfalls. We have impure hearts and thoughts. Thus, we become something that is displeasing to God. Once this happens, we must "trust in the Lord with all [our] heart and lean not to [our] own understanding, but in all thy ways acknowledge Him, and He shall direct [our] paths" (Proverbs 3:5). Then—and only then—will we see Him, and not only will we see Him and His will for our lives, but He will see us.

DAY 22

Don't Make Me Come Down this Mountain

DAILY READING:
I Timothy 2:2, Ephesians 5:21, Romans 13:1-7

And Moses turned and went down from the mount, and the two tables of the testimony were in his hand: the tables were written on both their sides; on the one side and on the other were they written. And the tables were the work of God, and the writing was the writing of God, graven upon the tables. And when Joshua heard the noise of the people as they shouted, he said unto Moses, "There is a noise of war in the camp." And he said, "It is not the voice of them that shout for mastery, neither is it the voice of them that cry for being overcome: but the noise of them that sing do I hear." And it came to pass, as soon as he came nigh unto the camp, that he saw the calf, and the dancing: and Moses' anger waxed hot, and he cast the tables out of his hands, and brake them beneath the mount.
—EXODUS 32:15-19

MOSES SPOKE WITH GOD LIKE a friend. He then led Israel to a close relationship with God, but there were still those who had difficulty following. Submission to someone who follows God will definitely assist us in achieving further intimacy with God. I would not have the relationship I have with God today had I not met a bishop who followed God. Wives are supposed to submit to their husbands as they follow Christ, and believers are to submit to their spiritual leaders as they follow Christ. Therefore, we should all exercise some submission in our lives. The Bible also teaches us to submit ourselves to one another (Ephesians 5:21). This means we should be serving and submitting to one another in the Lord, which improves our closeness with God for we are never any closer to God than we are to our neighbors.

The scripture tells us, "With man this is impossible, but with God all things are possible" (Luke 18:27). This tells me that humans will always have the potential to fail us. Moses came down from spending time with God to find that the people he had been leading had gone astray. Unfortunately, it is often the goats and not the sheep that bring out the true leader in us.

If we are not careful, the goats also have the ability to bring other things out of us. They can push us to our limits and cause us to disappoint God. Moses, in a sense, destroyed the work of God when he grew angry and shattered the tablets. Too often, we allow what other people do to cause us to fall. He carried the commandments, straight from God's finger, but he missed the point. What he had in his hands were the laws that would provide for a better relationship or covenant with God and his brother. In his frustration with his people's shortcomings, he disappointed both God and his fellow Israelites.

Likewise, we also carry the Word of God but still often miss the point—even some who preach and teach it. Again, we will never be any closer to God than we are to our brother (I John 4:20). Therefore, we must walk upright before our brothers and sisters, even when they fail, so that we do not exhibit another spirit contrary to God in our frustration with others.

YOUR CHALLENGE FOR DAY 22

Your challenge today is to place yourself in the presence of God and allow Him to become such a part of you that the imperfections you witness in others will not bother you and cause you to fall, but rather push you to be a better leader.

DAY 23

The Blessing of a More Intimate Relationship with God

DAILY READING:
Romans 8:28, I John 2:26-27, Psalm 73:27-28

But as it is written, eye hath not seen, nor ear heard, neither have entered into the heart of man, the things which God hath prepared for them that love Him. But God hath revealed them unto us by his Spirit: for the Spirit searcheth all things, yea, the deep things of God.
—I CORINTHIANS 2:9-10

BELIEVERS ARE ALWAYS ACCUSED OF being less intimate. Even the world, they have a better reputation with intimacy but are accused of having more "intimacy issues." This includes intimacy issues in marriages with spouses. People always want to know, how to get the fire back? How to keep the fire going? There is all this talk about intimacy? But why? The truth is, we will be clueless in our walk with God unless we grow in intimacy.

A good relationship with God will reveal friend from foe, direct our pathways, and allow us to live productive, fruitful lives. It may even bless us with material things, though that should not be our objective. We should never strive to be closer to God just because of the rewards we think we may get. That would be similar to getting married just because you want an expensive ring or a fancy wedding reception. No, we must love God because of who He is and not what we can get from Him.

Much like a marriage, there are benefits to a loving relationship with God. In a healthy marriage, we find happiness with the one we love, work together to become successful in our careers, bear children, and grow old in love. Likewise, there are some blessings that will come from loving God the right way instead of acting like His weekend lover. What He has prepared for those who love Him is unimaginable, unprecedented, and unmerited! It is so far beyond us that we cannot see it or hear it coming, and we know this because of His Spirit.

The text reads, "No eye ... but God has revealed them unto us." These are the ones who love Him, and we wait with such an expectation that God is going to do it, not because we see it, but because we can feel Him working. He has revealed to those of us who love Him that He is doing something and that this something is in our favor. To us, He will reveal what He has prepared.

This is the revelation of God, and He reveals it to believers for a reason and purpose. In other words, God births this in our minds, and after we accept Christ and the Holy Spirit sets up residence within us, that Spirit will reveal to us what God has in store. Why? Because we chose to love Him. There are plenty of things the Spirit helps us with once He takes residence within us, but our love for God is based on us. It is based on what we do and what we choose to give up. The scriptures teach, "If you love me, you will keep my commandments" (John 14:15).

When we sin and fall short of His glory, this says nothing about our salvation because the saving work is on Him, but it does leave our love for Him marked as questionable.

Your Challenge for Day 23

Your challenge today is to love God and allow your relationship with Him to become more and more intimate. You are to follow His commandments so that you may prove your love to Him. When you do this, He may well blow your mind with something unimaginable!

DAY 24

How Do I Cope with this Cave?

DAILY READING:
II Corinthians 4:8

*David therefore departed thence, and escaped to the cave Adullam: and
when his brethren and all his father's house heard it, they went down thither
to him. And everyone that was in distress, and everyone that was in debt,
and everyone that was discontented, gathered themselves unto him; and
he became a captain over them: and there were with him about 400 men.*
—I SAMUEL 22:1-2

W HEN WE ARE VERY CLOSE to God, we must be comfortable being
alone. People may not always be able to deal with us being so
spiritual. They may not be able deal with our closeness with God because
we will begin to do things His way. In other words, we may despise or
dislike things outside the will of God, but we must still be able to love
while living in holiness.

David, as anointed and gifted as he was, once found himself in a cave
instead of the palace. He was not there for punishment; he was seeking
escape. In the animal kingdom, there are classifications of cave dwellers,
those who frequently visit caves as guests. There are also cave lovers who

choose to live within them. Then, there are the incidentals; this is the category a lot of us may find ourselves in. These do not appreciate the cave, nor do they enjoy the habitation of the cave, yet they reside there until sunlight as a means of shelter and escape.

The incidentals allow the cave to protect them and keep them for a season. A bear, for example, only inhabits the cave for a season, to be protected from the elements. Too often, we spend too much time worried and wondering what got us into the cave instead of realizing the blessings that come from the cave itself.

Sometimes God puts us in a cave to allow us the opportunity to confront ourselves, away from the distractions of the outside world. Sometimes God maneuvers us through a cave experience to save us from ourselves. Case in point, I once visited a longtime friend of mine who was in the Intensive Care Unit. His hands were tied to the bed, and he was unable to speak or move. Because of his lifestyle, he found himself in a cave. As he lay there with no other ability but to listen, I asked him if I could pray. He mustered up what little strength he had and squeezed my hand in an effort to say a silent, "Yes. Please pray for me."

Sometimes a cave experience is exactly what it takes to make us yearn for the presence of God like we have never yearned for it before. It is the cave experience that will cause us to try God when we have never tried Him before.

In the cave, we also learn who our real friends are. Although David was in that cave with the worst of the worst, when it came time for battle, he knew who had his back. Most people will flee from us when we are in a cave, but sometimes it is best to be there so we can see who will stick with us even in the darkest of times.

A cave can also become a powerful place of prayer. Remember that some of the most powerful prayers in scripture came from David, while running from Saul and hiding from enemies and Daniel, in a den of hungry lions. Confinement allows—or perhaps forces—us to really get in touch with God. Sometimes we do not make time for God, so He forces us to make time for Him by putting us in isolation.

Your Challenge for Day 24

Your challenge today is to cope with the cave. If at all possible, you must seek out the blessings of the cave and remember that this is an incidental visit and not a permanent stay. When you learn what you need to learn and meet who you need to meet, then God will place you back in the palace.

DAY 25

Give God what is rightfully His

Daily Reading:
Luke 6:38, John 3:16,1 Peter 4:10

And the angel of the LORD called unto him out of Heaven, and said, "Abraham, Abraham!": and he said, "Here am I." And he said, "Lay not thine hand upon the lad, neither do thou anything unto him: for now I know that thou fearest God, seeing thou hast not withheld thy son, thine only son from me." And Abraham lifted up his eyes, and looked, and behold behind him a ram caught in a thicket by his horns: and Abraham went and took the ram, and offered him up for a burnt offering in the stead of his son. And Abraham called the name of that place Jehovah Jireh: as it is said to this day, In the mount of the LORD it shall be seen.
—Genesis 22:11-14

As I was reading this text, I discovered a reason beyond God's sovereignty that allows Him to ask of us what He will. First, He opens Himself up for us to ask of Him what we will. Jesus stated, "And whatsoever ye shall ask in my name, that will I do, that the Father may be glorified in the Son" (John 14:13). He can ask what He will of us because He gave us the best Heaven had to offer the best He had - ALL

He had. He sacrificed His Son for a world that was headed for Hell then and remains. He created us to be in perfect covenant with Him, and His preferred option to save us once sin entered the world was to give up His only begotten Son.

As I have already established, intimacy requires sacrifice. It entails having the same sacrificial love for God that He has for us. Thus, when God asks us to give up our guilty pleasures, our time, or our money, who are we to argue and deny Him what He asks for? For the record, Abraham was not the only one who was asked to give his child to God. In reality, God has asked all of us to train our children up in the Lord. He has asked of us that we teach them the God we know and trust; in this way, He asks for our seed just as He asked for Abraham's by testing his faith.

Has your relationship with God impacted your child? If you had your child or children out of wedlock, did your child do the same, or did you teach them to recognize right from wrong and to learn from your past mistakes? Whether we are willing to admit it or not, generational curses are not always the result of the devil's tight grip on our lineage. Oftentimes, these occur because we fail to give our children to God, to be obedient to Him when it costs us. If we teach our children in the way of the Lord rather than the way of man, they will be able to grow beyond our mistakes instead of repeating them and passing them on.

If we cannot be the salt of the Earth, as we are called to be, the least we can do is be the salt of our homes. In our own homes, our own families, we can impact our loved ones so that they can come to know the God we serve and teach future generations to do the same.

YOUR CHALLENGE FOR DAY 25

Your challenge today is to train up your children and give them to God, despite the mistakes you or your parents or guardians have made. Remember that delayed obedience is disobedience; the longer you wait, the more difficult this will be for you and for your kids.

DAY 26

He only deserves the best

DAILY READING:
James 2:23; 4:8-10, John 14:22-23

And the angel of the LORD called unto him out of Heaven, and said, "Abraham, Abraham!": and he said, "Here am I." And he said, "Lay not thine hand upon the lad, neither do thou anything unto him: for now I know that thou fearest God, seeing thou hast not withheld thy son, thine only son from me." And Abraham lifted up his eyes, and looked, and behold behind him a ram caught in a thicket by his horns: and Abraham went and took the ram, and offered him up for a burnt offering in the stead of his son. And Abraham called the name of that place Jehovah Jireh: as it is said to this day, In the mount of the LORD it shall be seen.
—GENESIS 22:11-14

ABRAHAM'S WILLINGNESS TO GIVE ISAAC up to God is an example of true sacrifice. We must be willing to give up to God whatever He asks for. Not only should we give God our children, but we should also offer ourselves to Him: everything that is within us, since He was willing to give a part of Himself to us through Christ. The idea of the only begotten Son is that He gave of His very self. When we do this for God,

He will bless us in return. God is true to the promises in the Bible. I am persuaded to believe that He *wants* to give to us when we honor our part of the covenant or relationship.

How can we expect God to open doors for us if we aren't willing to give Him our all? How can we expect Him to open doors for our children to get into college or protect them in the streets if we aren't willing to give them over to God's will and train them up to know Him? When we give our children to God, He has to protect them from gang violence, HIV, or whatever is in the world because they belong to Him. Just as He did for Abraham, He will provide a ram in the thicket. He will spare our Isaacs if we are willing to give our children up to Him, to become His responsibility. Rest assured He can raise them better than we ever could anyway!

When we give God all that's within us in ministry, He has to open doors for us because that means we have given our hearts, souls, and minds to His service. It may be our names on the office door, but those office doors are in His churches! Let us never forget that God did not provide for Abraham because He and Abraham had such a remarkable relationship. Rather, He provided for Abraham because Abraham was faithful on his end. Likewise, if you are faithful to God, He will be faithful to you.

Because Abraham believed God, he was counted as righteous, and God considered him a friend. This was not just applicable for Abraham; it is also obtainable for us today. We, too, can believe God and be counted as His friends. I believe this teaching—that God is our friend—has been lost throughout the years because too many people try to get close to God simply to see what they can get out of it, not for the sake of having an intimate relationship with our Creator.

Your Challenge for Day 26

Ask yourself if things are your motivation when it comes to God. Your challenge this day is not to beat God at giving, because you never will. Instead, just give Him your all and be a faithful steward of what He has entrusted to your care.

DAY 27

The Danger of Looking Back

DAILY READING:
Luke 9:57-62, Luke 17:26-35, Philippians 3:12-14

But his wife looked back from behind him, and she became a pillar of salt.
—GENESIS 19:26

A S I READ THIS SCRIPTURE, the Lord revealed to me that even today, there is a danger in looking back. This principle is both implied and taught in scripture. God told Lot not to look back because He did not want Lot to be consumed with the sins of the past. Likewise, if you continue to look back instead of forward, your past may consume or destroy you.

We cannot walk this Christian walk in retrospect, or we will be consumed. We should not be afraid of our pasts, but we should not dwell there any longer than necessary. God warned Lot and his family that they should run for their lives, without looking back. To live a successful life, we must look forward. We cannot become stagnate or stuck or sit on your laurels, bragging or languishing about what we used to do or who we used to be. Truth be told, not only will constantly looking back consume us, but it may keep us from doing anything new for the Lord. If we are too busy talking about what God used to do through us, we might miss the chance to sing, pray, or preach, as if God is not the same, yesterday, today, and forevermore.

It was not Lot's problem that the city was being consumed, for he was one of the few faithful with the opportunity to be saved. Even though it was not Lot's mess that he was leaving behind, that mess would have consumed him—just as it did his wife—if he had looked back. We can be consumed or destroyed by the messes others make. For this reason, ungodly relationships should be left behind as a thing of the past, and ungodly places should never be revisited. Although we are new, changed, and delivered through Christ, the messy lives of others can be very detrimental to your growth.

Trust me: If we try to mingle and hang in the balance between where God wants to take us and where you have been, if we try to hang on to the people and things that we should not be clinging to, we are just moments from being consumed. If we are looking for change, looking to improve ourselves, we need to get out before it's too late! As Lot's wife quickly discovered, once we are consumed by the things and people that were pleasing to us in the past, we will reach a point of ultimate destruction—a point where it is impossible to be restored. If we do not move ahead and insist on looking back, not only will God leave us salt-like, but just plain salty.

YOUR CHALLENGE FOR DAY 27

Your challenge today is to move before you are consumed. This means you must let go of people, places, and things for the sake of your healthy spirituality. If God permits, you may be able to go back and restore them, but if this is your time to move, you should move without hesitation, or you are doomed to be consumed.

DAY 28

Opening the Door to a Higher Standard

DAILY READING:
Colossians 3:16, Ephesians 5:26, John 15:7

And the Word was made flesh, and dwelt among us, (and we beheld His glory, the glory as of the only begotten of the Father,) full of grace and truth.
—JOHN 1:14

IT IS MY PRAYER THAT as you have been reading this devotional, you have been reading it along with your Bible. Every statement herein can be validated by the Word of God. Without the Word, we have no principles by which to live. While the language is ancient, the "thee" and "thou" that God spoke with in His Word still refers to us, and we live on the same planet. These same principles apply to our lives today, and we would be utterly lost without them. Much of the world is adrift because they refuse to recognize the Word of God as any authority.

The Word was made flesh, meaning it was incarnate. When the Word was made flesh, it allowed us the opportunity to apply the Word—and not only to apply it, but to apply it while living in the flesh. When the Word became flesh, it did not bring the standard down; rather, He gave us the capability to rise up to meet the standard.

Before this, it may have been arguable that such a feat could not possibly be accomplished, but Christ made the standard accessible, even for sinners such as us. If the Word was made flesh, then it became obtainable to us in the flesh. Because the Word was made flesh, we can apply it to our bodies and call ourselves to line up with the Word—not only because the Word was made flesh, but also because He died in the flesh and was raised by his Father. Our transgressions were put on His tab; our iniquities and the chastisement of our peace has been placed on his record.

YOUR CHALLENGE FOR DAY 28

Your challenge today is not to be intimidated by the Word or even what the Word requires of you. Rather, you should embrace His Word and allow it to become a regular part of your life and your walk with God. Remember that the Bible tells us we cannot live without it: "Man shall not live by bread alone but by every word that proceedeth out of the mouth of God." (Matthew 4:4).

DAY 29

If You Close the Door, He Will Open Doors

DAILY READING:
James 5:16, I Thessalonians 5:17-18, Luke 18:1

And when thou prayest, thou shalt not be as the hypocrites are: for they love to pray standing in the synagogues and in the corners of the streets, that they may be seen of men. Verily I say unto you, they have their reward. But thou, when thou prayest, enter into thy closet, and when thou hast shut thy door, pray to thy Father which is in secret; and thy Father which seeth in secret shall reward thee openly.
—MATTHEW 6:5-6

I T IS IMPOSSIBLE TO HAVE a more intimate relationship with God without an active prayer life. We must have constant communication with God if we want to be intimate with Him. It is commonly known that without good communication in our marriages, our love lives and intimacy with our partner will never be successful or happy or fulfilling. Likewise, how can we be intimate with God if we never speak to Him? Prayer is a way to do all we are striving to do: It encompasses self-denial and the destroying of the flesh, and if it is done correctly, it will benefit us as well as our brothers and sisters.

The more intimate our prayer life, the more rewards we store up in Heaven. Scripture tells us, "Take heed that you do not your alms before men, to be seen of them: otherwise, ye have no reward of your Father which is in Heaven" (Matthew 6:1). We should not seek to have an intimate prayer life only for reward, though, for there are no spiritual deposits in your heavenly bank account if you pray in this manner.

Remember, if we shut the wrong doors, He will open the right ones. When we close the door and pray in private—really talk to God—we should imagine that we are closing the doors on hypocrisy, vainglory, and man-pleasing because God sees what we think and strive for in secret. He watches our secret lives more than that which we put on display. God takes inventory of our quiet time and our private reflections to see if we are worthy of His blessings. If we are worthy for Him to open and shed light on our private lives and we prove to be wholeheartedly His, then He will reward us openly. God does not like to bless in secret, for He wants everyone to see His blessings, but He cannot attach Himself to anyone who refuses to be His. Would we feel loved by our spouses if they only spoke to us once a week in front of others? No way! Likewise, if we only pray on Sunday mornings, especially just for show, we must ask ourselves if we are truly His.

YOUR CHALLENGE FOR DAY 29

Your challenge today is simple: Pray and pray without ceasing. Close the door and make a daily appointment in prayer! Pray for yourself, to repent, pray for your family, for a better relationship with God, and pray for your neighbors and your brothers and sisters. Do not shut the doors on Him, but close the door to spend intimate time with Him in prayer.

DAY 30

After Knowledge Comes Accountability

DAILY READING:
Hebrews 10:26

*For if we sin willfully after that we have received the knowledge
of the truth, there remaineth no more sacrifice for sins.*
—HEBREWS 10:26

ONGRATULATIONS! YOU HAVE MADE IT through all thirty days in your quest for a more intimate relationship with God. This has likely not made your journey easier, but more challenging. You have been challenged to seek and search God's best, you have been encouraged to be better socially and spiritually, to love your neighbor, and to properly deal with and handle your enemy. You have also been given instructions on how to forgive and how to deal with life when wrongs are committed against you. You have been instructed to walk after the Spirit and not the flesh, to keep the commandments of God, and to be better person in your home and marriage. We have discussed how model believers should act, how they should walk, and how they should get back up when they fall. Now, on this fortieth day, the best advice and instruction I can give you is to apply the Word of God. I implore you to continue growing in God and never become stuck or stagnant in Him or allow your gifts and callings to go unused and unheeded.

You must now apply what you know, for the excuse that you do not know or that you are not aware of what you should be doing is no longer valid if you have read these pages. Now, you will be held accountable for practicing what you have learned here, in these pages and in the pages of God's Word through your daily readings. Hopefully, your devotional life has grown, along with your spirituality. Hopefully, you have overcome some of the obstacles of your Christian walk in the past thirty days.

YOUR CHALLENGE FOR DAY 30

Your challenge today is simply to apply what you know and pray for me as I pray for you, that we all might be better for Christ.

Peace and love, my brothers and sisters,
Evangelist J.L. Turner

Day 1

- » *Philippians 3:8*
- » *John 14:22-23*
- » *Hebrews 12:6*

Day 2

- » *Romans 13:10*
- » *Psalm 73:27-28*
- » *Ephesians 1:4*
- » *Matthew 22:37-40*

Day 3

- » *Philippians 2:1-4*
- » *Romans 12:9-10*
- » *Proverbs 18:24*
- » *John 15:12-17*

Day 4

- » *Philippians 3:8*
- » *Revelations 3:20*
- » *John 14:22-23*
- » *I Peter 4:1-2*

Day 5

- » *Isaiah 63:7-10*
- » *James 4:8-10*
- » *I Peter 4:1-2*

Day 6

- » *Romans 8:1*
- » *Romans 12:2*
- » *II Corinthians 5:17*

Day 7

- » *Psalm 73:27-28*
- » *James 4:8-10*
- » *Romans 6:1-10*

Day 8

- » *I Peter 4:1-2*
- » *I Corinthians 15:31-34*
- » *Philippians 2:1-4*

Day 11

- » *Romans 12:9-10*
- » *Proverbs 18:24*
- » *Psalm 23:5*

Day 12

- » *Hebrews 4:14-16*
- » *Hebrews 11:6*
- » *Psalm 121:1*
- » *Galatians 6:7-9*
- » *II Chronicles 7:14*

Day 13

- » *I John 2:26-27*
- » *Romans 8:14-15*
- » *Isaiah 63:10*

Day 14

- » *Joel 2:28*
- » *Galatians 6:7-9*
- » *Galatians 5:19-22*

Day 15

- » *Matthew 3:2*
- » *Luke 5:32*
- » *Luke 13:5*
- » *Luke 15:7*
- » *Revelations 3:19*

Day 16

- » *John 15:12-17*
- » *II Timothy 4:5*
- » *Philippians 3:8*

Day 17

- » *Psalm 37*
- » *Psalm 27:14*

Day 18

- » *Romans 5:6-10*
- » *Proverbs 18:24*
- » *Isaiah 41:8*
- » *I Timothy 2:5*

Day 19

- » *Matthew 6:12, 14*
- » *Matthew 18:21-35*
- » *Luke 6:37*

Day 20

- » *Philippians 3:8*

- » *Galatians 6:7-9*

Day 21

- » *I Corinthians 12:4-7, 11-12, 18, 24-27*
- » *Romans 17:9-10*

Day 22

- » *Psalm 139:13-14*
- » *Philippians 4:13*

Day 23

- » *II Chronicles 16:9*
- » *Philippians 4:8-9*
- » *Proverbs 3:5*
- » *Proverbs 23:74*

Day 24

- » *Romans 8:28*
- » *I John 2:26-27*
- » *Psalm 73:27-28*

Day 25

- » *II Corinthians 4:8*

Day 26

- » *James 2:23*
- » *James 4:8-10*
- » *John 14:22-23*

Day 27

- » *Hebrews 12:14*
- » *II Corinthians 7:1*
- » *Isaiah 35:8*

Day 28

- » *Proverbs 18:24*
- » *Romans 13:10*
- » *II Corinthians 5:14-15*

Day 29

- » *James 5:16*
- » *I Thessalonians 5:17-18*
- » *Luke 18:1*

Day 30

- » *Hebrews 10:26*

Look for Evangelist Turner's second book:

Rise Above it:
The Christian response vs. The Christian reaction